Henry Martyn Burt

Burt's Guide through the Connecticut Valley to the White Mountains

And the River Saguenay

Henry Martyn Burt

Burt's Guide through the Connecticut Valley to the White Mountains
And the River Saguenay

ISBN/EAN: 9783337209759

Printed in Europe, USA, Canada, Australia, Japan

Cover: Foto ©Andreas Hilbeck / pixelio.de

More available books at **www.hansebooks.com**

THROUGH THE

CONNECTICUT VALLEY

TO THE

WHITE MOUNTAINS

AND THE

RIVER SAGUENAY.

By HENRY M. BURT,

EDITOR OF THE NEW ENGLAND HOMESTEAD.

SPRINGFIELD, MASS.:
NEW ENGLAND PUBLISHING COMPANY.
1874.

HENRY M. BURT, PRINTER,
Springfield, Mass.

WHY?

In presenting this book to the public, it has been the aim of the writer, to awaken an increased interest in the beautiful and grand in nature, and to direct attention to the fairest and loveliest regions of New England, that the seeker after health and pleasure, might obtain a more perfect knowledge of that which lies almost at his own door. Occasional anecdotes have been gathered from the way-side and here presented, to enliven and relieve the monotony of description, as too much of even the best, never fails to weary the keenest of tastes. It has been truly said that,

>A little nonsense now and then,
>Is relished by the best of men.

The engraving for this book has mostly been done by Mr. E. Kingsley, of the Star Printing Company of Northampton, and by Milton Bradley & Co. of Springfield, well known in their profession. The humerous illustrations are by Palmer Cox, a rising California artist and author.

The Guide is at your service, Reader, and it is hoped you will find in it a help to your enjoyment of a tour through New England, where it is confidently believed you can find increased health and a pleasant life-long remembrance.

HOW TO GO.

The tourist has the choice of several routes from New York to the White Mountains. From New York he can take the cars at 3 P. M., for Springfield, and reach the latter place at 7.50; remain over night, and proceed north at 8 next morning. Or he can take, in New York, the New Haven and Northampton car, attached to the same train, proceed to New Haven, and from that point pass over the New Haven and Northampton Railroad to Easthampton, or Northampton; remain over night, and take the train north which leaves Springfield at 8 A. M. At Easthampton, Mr. Hill, of Hill's Mansion House, will take the best of care of guests. The 3 P. M. boat from Peck Slip, and 3.15 from 23d street, East River, to New Haven, makes connections with the train, at New Haven, which arrives in Springfield the same evening. This is a favorite route with many, as it gives an afternoon sail on the Sound.

The train leaving Springfield at 8 A. M., arrives at the Fabyan House, within four miles of the Crawford House, at 5.30 P. M. Stages run to the Crawford House on arrival of the train. The Fabyan House is, also, within six miles of the Mt. Washington Railway. Stages run between these places, as they also do between the Crawford House and the Mt. Washington Railway.

Tourists going direct to the Profile House leave the cars at Littleton and proceed south, eleven miles, by stage, arriving at 8 P. M.

Regular lines of stages run between all the Hotels, and also between the Hotels and the Railroad.

After the 15th of July, the Mt. Washington Railway makes two trips daily between the base and summit. Leaves the base at 10.30 A. M., and 5.30 P. M. Returning, leaves the summit at 8 A. M. and 2 P. M.

For Quebec, the 8 A. M. train from Springfield makes connection with the train at Sherbrook, Canada, on the Grand Trunk, which arrives at Point Levi, opposite Quebec, at 10 P. M., same day.

For River Saguenay, leave Quebec by steamer on Tuesday, Wednesday, Thursday, Friday, and Saturday, at 7 A. M., on arrival of the steamer leaving Montreal at 7, the previous evening. The Saguenay trip occupies forty-eight hours.

RAILROAD FARES.

New York to Profile House,	-	-	$11.25
" " " Fabyan House,	-	-	10.25
" " " Crawford House,	-	-	11.25
" " " Lake Memphremagog,	-	-	10.40
" " " Montreal,	-	-	12.00
" " " Quebec,	-	-	14.50
Springfield " Profile House,	-	-	9.25
" " Fabyan House,	-	-	8.25
" " Crawford House,	-	-	9.25
" " Lake Memphremagog,	-	-	8.30
" " Montreal,	-	-	9.50
" " Quebec,	-	-	12.00

STAGE FARES.

Crawford House to Profile House,	-	$4.00
" " " Glen House,	-	5.00
" " " Fabyan House,	-	1.00
" " " Mt. Washington Railway,	-	3.00
" " " " " " and return,		4.00

Stages for all Hotels make close connection with all trains on Mt. Washington Railway, to and from the summit.

MT. WASHINGTON RAILWAY.

Base to Summit,	$3.00
Summit to Base,	3.00
Base to Summit and return,	4.00
Extra charge for trunks each way, about	2.00

HOTEL CHARGES.

All the first class Hotels in the Mountains charge from $4.00 to $4.50 per day. At the Summit House on Mt. Washington the charge is $6.00 per day, or $4.50 for supper, lodging and breakfast. Dinner $2.00.

TABLE OF DISTANCES.

N. Y., N. H. & Hartford R. R.

0	New York.
11	Williams' Bridge.
14	Mt. Vernon.
15	Pelhamville.
17	New Rochelle.
19	Larch. Manor.
21	Mamaroneck.
22	Harrison.
24	Rye.
26	Port Chester.
28	Greenwich.
30	Cos Cob Bridge.
30	Riverside.
34	Stamford.
37	Norton.
38	Darien.
39	Five Mile River.
42	South Norwalk.
45	Westport.
47	Green's Farms.
49	Southport.
51	Fairfield.
56	Bridgeport.
59	Stratford.
61	Naugatuck R. Junction.
64	Milford.
71	West Haven.
73	New Haven.
80	North Haven.
85	Wallingford.
88	Yalesville.
91	Meriden.
98	Berlin.
104	Newington.
109	Hartford.
115	Windsor.
121	Windsor Locks.
122	Warehouse Point.
127	Thompsonville.
131	Longmeadow.
135	Springfield.

Connecticut River R. R.

0	Springfield.
4	Chicopee Junction.
7	Willimansett.
8	Holyoke.
13	Smith's Ferry.
15	Mount Tom.
18	Easthampton.
17	Northampton.
21	Hatfield.
24	North Hatfield.
26	Whately.
28	South Deerfield.
33	Deerfield.
36	Greenfield.
43	Bernardston.
50	South Vernon.

Central Vermont R. R.

0	South Vernon.
5	Vernon.
10	Brattleboro.
19	Putney.
30	Westminster.
34	Bellows Falls.
42	Charlestown.
47	North Charlestown.
52	Claremont.
60	Windsor.
64	Hartland.
69	North Hartland.
74	White River Junction.
94	Royalton.
99	Bethel.
127	Northfield.
138	Montpelier.
148	Waterbury.
170	Essex Junction.
176	Burlington.
195	St. Albans.
237	St. Johns.
259	Montreal.

Boston, Lowell & Nashua R. R.

0	Boston.
26	Lowell.
40	Nashua.
57	Manchester.
75	Concord.

Boston, Concord & Montr'l R. R.

27	Laconia.
29	Lake Village.
33	Weirs.
51	Plymouth.
84	Haverhill.
94	Wells River.
0	Wells River.
20	Littleton.
31	Profile House.
27	Wing Road.
29	Bethlehem.
34	Twin Mountain.
38	Fabyan's.
42	Crawford House.
44	Mt. Washington R. R.
47	" " Summit.
55	Glen House.

Eastern Rail Road.

0	Boston.
36	Newburyport.
56	Portsmouth.
67	Conway Junction.

CONWAY DIVISION.

0	Conway Junction.
6	Great Falls.
31	Wolfboro' Junction.
65	Conway.
71	North Conway.
91	Upper Bartlett.
121	Crawford House.
134	Mt. Washington Summit.

Conn., & Passumpsic R., R. R.

0	White River Junction.
5	Norwich.
10	Pompanoosuc.
15	Thetford.
17	North Thetford.
22	Fairlee.
29	Bradford.
33	South Newbury.
36	Newbury.
40	Wells River.
48	McIndoes.
51	Barnet.
58	Passumpsic.
61	St. Johnsbury.
64	St. Johnsbury Center.
69	Lyndonville.
77	West Burke.
86	South Barton.
90	Barton.
96	Barton Landing.
100	Coventr.
105	Newport.
111	Stanstead Junction.
115	Smith's Mills.
118	Libby's Mills.
124	Ayer's Flats.
126	Massawippi.
133	North Hatley.
142	Lennoxville.
145	Sherbrooke.
170	Richmond.
266	Quebec.

Southeastern [Canada] R. R.

0	Newport.
31	Richford.
43	Southon Junction.
65	West Farham.
79	St. Johns.
101	Montreal.

THE CONTENTS.

BY CHAPTERS.

	PAGES.
New York to New Haven.	9—22
New Haven to Hartford.	22—36
Hartford to Springfield.	36—59
Springfield to Northampton.	59—86
New Haven to Williamsburg.	86—102
Northampton to Greenfield.	103—135
Greenfield to Brattleboro.	135—142
Brattleboro to Bellows' Falls.	142—167
Bellows Falls to White River Junction.	167—177
White River Junction to Newport.	177—201
Lake Memphremagog,	202—227
White Mountains.	228—274
Quebec.	275—281
Down the St. Lawrence.	281—288
The River Saguenay.	290—297

THE GUIDE.

THE fertility and beauty of the Connecticut Valley have long been known to the favored few, and poets and artists have given the world glimpses of its salient points, but it was not until quite a recent period that its charming and matchless characteristics became known to the many. The extension of more rapid and comfortable modes of travel has opened the doors to this elysian field, and thousands come with the recurring period of foliage and flowers, to worship at the shrine of beauty found in lofty mountains, broad meadows, and a majestic river. While the noble Connecticut is the Rhine of New England, the region of its source is the Switzerland of America, and year by year the pilgrims to this favored land journey thither in search of rest and inspiration.

Leaving the Grand Central Depot, at 42d street,

New York, the traveler enters upon his journey. The ride over the New York and New Haven Railroad, a distance of 74 miles, is one of the most agreeable that can be taken by rail. Elegant private residences crown the hill-tops on every hand, evidences of wealth and refinement, while the views of the Sound, at various points, dotted with the sails of busy commerce, and of the shores of Long Island in the distance, give pleasing variety to the scene. Many places along the route are of historic interest, where were enacted in the Revolution deeds that will be ever memorable. These villages have been built, or greatly improved, by persons doing business in New York, who have sought homes in these quiet rural scenes near the great city. The beautiful lawns and groves that are passed are in refreshing contrast to the paved and dusty streets just left behind.

HARLEM.

Five miles north of 42d street is Harlem, once a suburban village, but now part of the Great Metropolis. Crossing Harlem River, the villages of Mott Haven, Morrisania, and Fordham are passed before reaching Williams' Bridge, where the Harlem Railroad branches to the left and pursues a northerly route through the country, parallel with the Hudson River.

NEW ROCHELLE.

This beautiful town, situated nearly eighteen miles from New York, was settled by Huguenots, from

Rochelle, in France. For several years it was the residence of Thomas Paine, who died in 1809. He was buried here upon what was formerly a part of his own estate. The monument erected to his memory bears the following inscription, in accordance with his own request: "Thomas Paine, author of Common Sense, died June 8, 1809, aged 72 years." Paine was the son of an English Quaker, and coming to this country in 1774, he settled in Philadelphia. In 1776 he wrote a pamphlet entitled Common Sense, in which he urged the separation of the colonies from the mother country. It met with universal favor, and, more than any one thing, brought the people to the point of resisting British tyranny. The pamphlet won him the friendship of Washington, Franklin, Dr. Rush, and other distinguished American leaders, and Congress acknowledged his services by appointing him Secretary to the Committee on Foreign Affairs. He was the author of the often quoted line, "these are the times that try men's souls," which appeared in the Crisis, another Revolutionary pamphlet published by him. In 1787 he visited France, went from there to England, and returned to the United States in 1802, settling in New York. The Quakers refusing him a place of interment in their grounds, which favor he requested before his death, he was buried on his farm in New Rochelle. William Cobbett, the English reformer, who visited this country and wrote a biography of Paine, disinterred his remains and took them to England. The monument erected to his memory stands within a few feet of where he was first buried.

THE STATE LINE.

The stations of Mamaroneck, Rye, and Port Chester, are passed before reaching the boundary line between New York and Connecticut. The latter place is situated at the mouth of Bryam River, after crossing which, the tourist enters Connecticut.

GREENWICH.

Soon after passing Port Chester, and 31 miles from New York, will be seen the village of Greenwich, situated on a hill, about a mile north of the railroad. It contains some elegant residences and two large churches—Congregational and Episcopalian, built of stone. The Congregational church stands in a conspicuous place, and its spire can be seen for several miles on either side of the village. The Episcopal church stands almost on the brow of the hill further to the east. The view of the Sound and Long Island from the village is extensive and picturesque.

OLD PUT RIDING DOWN THE ROCKS.

This place was made famous by one of those daring exploits of Gen. Israel Putnam, in the Revolution, which so distinguished him for bravery. Putnam was stationed here with 150 men and two cannon, which were without drag ropes or horses, to check the advance of the British, under Tryon, who was making an incursion into Connecticut with 1500 men. Tryon sent a party of dragoons, supported

by infantry, to charge up the hill and dislodge Putnam's little band. A spirited firing was kept up until Putnam, deeming further resistance useless, ordered his men to retreat into the swamp on the east, beyond the reach of the cavalry. He kept his position until his men were safely away, and then, just as the British troopers were riding down upon him from the west, sure of their coveted prize, Putnam put spurs to his fleet horse and rode at a breakneck speed to the east, down the stone steps that had been constructed for the use of the people who ascended the hill to attend church. When the British came to the spot Putnam had just left, their horses stopped with fright, and the intrepid hero made good his escape. A volley was fired at him and one bullet passed through his hat. The General, still unharmed, kept on to Stamford, where he raised a larger force and returned and fell upon Tryon's rear, then on retreat, and captured 38 prisoners and considerable ammunition. The next day he made an exchange of prisoners with Tryon, who sent him a new suit of clothes, including a hat, to take the place of the one that had been pierced with bullets, a compliment for his bravery and humanity. A man who stood near Putnam, says the historian, when he made the fearful plunge down the rocks, said he was "cursing the British terribly." The hill, at this point, is a hundred feet high and quite steep. A public road has been cut through the rocks, just north of where this daring exploit occurred, leading to Coscob. A little way east of the Greenwich depot the railroad passes through the same ledge, and the locality can be seen from the cars. A few rods east of the Episcopal church, on the brow of the hill, will be noticed a large, square, white house. This stands about ten rods north of where the stone steps were located. They have been removed, but the place still bears the name of "Put's Hill." Soon after leaving Greenwich, the road crosses Mianus River upon a draw bridge, forty feet above the water, where the trains stop, in compliance with the laws of the State. The village of Coscob will be noticed a mile north of the railroad.

STAMFORD.

Crossing Stamford River the express trains make their first stop at the beautiful town of Stamford, 35 miles from New York, one of the neatest on the whole line. This place is noted for its wide and shady streets, elegant private residences and great wealth. Many people live here who do business in New York. There are four public parks in the town, and the drives over the summits north and east of the village, from which an extensive view is had, are unsurpassed. There are eight churches in the town—one Congregational, Presbyterian, two Episcopal, Baptist, Universalist, Methodist, and one Catholic. Population 10,000. The next way station is Darien, a small and quiet village, situated upon a stream that falls into the sound.

NORWALK.

Norwalk, the second stopping place for express trains, is celebrated for its oysters and hats. Some three to five hundred hands are employed in the oyster business and it is estimated that nearly $500,000 annually are received for the sale of oysters that are sent to other parts of the country.

There is no other town on the sound so extensively engaged in this business, Fair Haven standing next. The manufacture of hats is quite extensive and a large number of hands are employed. The village at the depot is known as South Norwalk, and has been built since the completion of the railroad; the old village, or Norwalk proper, is located about a mile and a half north of the railroad and is connected with the south village by a horse railroad, built by the late Le Grand Lockwood, who resided here. The streets are wide, and the large shade trees and elegant residences give the appearance of neatness and comfort. There are nine churches in the two villages. The hills on the west, north and east, afford excellent sites for dwellings, and on many of them are extensive and costly edifices. Norwalk was almost totally destroyed by the British and Tories, who burnt it July 11, 1779. The loss estimated by a committee appointed by the General Assembly, exceeded $116,000. The population of the town is about 10,000. The Danbury and Norwalk Railroad extends from the south village to Danbury, a distance of 24 miles. Leaving Norwalk the railroad crosses the draw bridge forty feet above the water, where that sad disaster occurred to the express train, which run into the open draw, several years since, killing a large number of passengers. Great precaution has since been taken to prevent a repetition of such accidents. Before reaching the next station for express trains, the beautiful towns of Westport, Southport, and Fairfield are passed.

North of Southport station is the Pequot swamp, where that once great and powerful tribe of Indians, in 1637, made their last stand against Connecticut and Massachusetts troops. Fairfield was burnt July 7, 1779, by Gov. Tryon, who sailed the previous day from New Haven. This was one of the most destructive conflagrations occasioned by the British, during the Revolution. Two hundred houses were burnt just at night, by the order of Tryon. A thunder storm over spread the heavens soon after the village was set on fire, and the whole scene was one of terrible grandeur.

BRIDGEPORT.

Bridgeport, 57 miles from New York, is a thriving city of 20,000 inhabitants. At the close of the Revolution there were less than a dozen houses where the city now stands. An extensive business is done here in manufacturing the Wheeler & Wilson and the Howe Sewing Machines. There are 15 churches in the city. The South church, which was built in 1861, will seat 1,000 persons, and its spire is 209 feet high.

Charles S. Stratton, better known as Gen. Tom Thumb, was born in Bridgeport, Jan. 4, 1832. He weighed nine pounds at birth, and continued to grow until seven months old, when, from some unexplained cause, he ceased to increase in size and weight. His hight is 28 inches. In 1844 he visited Europe and has had the honor of appearing before nearly all the crowned heads of the old world.

In 1853 he was married to Miss Lavinia Warren, a dwarf of about his own stature. The parents of the General have had two other children who have reached the usual hight.

The Naugatuck Railroad, extending to Winsted, 62 miles, and the Housatonic, extending to Pittsfield, 110 miles, intersect the New York and New Haven Railroad, the former at this place, and the latter at Naugatuck Junction, east of Housatonic River. The trains on this road run into Bridgeport.

Stratford, about four miles from Bridgeport, is a pleasant, rural village. The principal street, about one mile in length, is ornamented with fine shade trees. Gen. Wooster, killed at Ridgefield in the Revolution, was a native of this town.

MILFORD.—SOLDIERS' MONUMENT.

Milford, 65 miles from New York and 8 from Bridgeport, is a quiet but beautiful town. It contains some elegant private residences, and the large elms which line the principal streets give the place a pleasant and ancient appearance. In Jan, 1777, two hundred American soldiers, in a sick and dying condition, were brought from a British prison ship at New York, and suddenly cast on the shore near this place. They were cared for by the inhabitants of the village, but in less than a month 46 of them died and were burried in one common grave. Near the railroad, in the old cemetery, east of the depot, a freestone monument, 30 feet high, has been erected to their memory. It can be seen from the cars, north of the track.

As the traveler approaches New Haven from New York, he will notice West Rock, to the north, which is from three to four hundred feet high.

WEST ROCK.—THE JUDGES' CAVE.

On the summit of West Rock is the celebrated Judges' Cave, where the regicides, Goffe and Whalley, two of the judges who condemned King Charles I, concealed themselves when pursued by the King's officers. It is not a cave, strictly speaking, but an aperture in the rocks, which afforded shelter to the regicides. Upon the rocks are engraved these words, "Opposition to tyrants is obedience to God." Goffe

EAST ROCK.

and Whalley, previous to their concealment on West Rock, resided in New Haven, but their arrest being ordered, they were obliged to flee from the city, and afterward lived in Hadley, Mass.

East Rock, two miles east of West Rock, and a mile north-east of New Haven, is frequently visited. It is about the same hight as West Rock, and the view of New Haven and the Sound from its summit is grand and beautiful. A better view of East Rock from the cars is had after the train leaves New Haven for Hartford and Springfield, a short distance out of the city.

NEW HAVEN.

New York, 74. White Mountains, 254; Lake Memphremagog, 293; Montreal, 374; Quebec, 454 miles.

ON approaching New Haven, the tourist will observe the church spires on the Public Square, the City Hall, and other public buildings on the left. To the right is Long Wharf, and the Light House in the distance. Chapel street, on which a larger part of the mercantile business is done, passes over the railroad, north of the depot. To reach the Public Square and the College buildings, take Chapel Street, and a walk of five minutes, to the west, will bring you to them. They are located in the best part of the city. The magnificent elms, overarching the walks, and the general beauty and neatness of the city at once attract the attention of the visitor, leaving an agreeable impression of the place upon his mind.

New Haven was settled in 1638, by a company of exiled Englishmen from London and vicinity, who had been merchants, and it is said that this was the most wealthy colony that had come to this country. The city was originally laid out in a plot half a mile square. It is beautifully situated on an extensive plain at the head of the bay, which extends four miles in from the Sound. North of the city are high lands, overlooking it and the Sound, the most prominent of which are East and West Rocks. Its public squares and ancient elms add greatly to the beauty of the city, giving it an appearance unlike any other place in this country, and as one walks underneath those living arches of green, it is suggested that New Haven is truly entitled to the name of "Elm City," by which it is familiarly known.

The view in Temple street, which extends through the Public Square, north and south, is particularly striking. For a long distance the broad elms form a magnificent arch, more perfect and beautiful than could be made by the hand of man. The view selected for illustration by the artist is from the center of the Green, looking north.

TEMPLE STREET, NEW HAVEN, CONN.

The Public Square, or Green, as it is called, situated between Chapel and Elm Streets, on the south and north, and College and Church Streets, on the west and east, contains 16 acres. Temple Street extends through it from north to south, and the elms are so large that a complete arch is formed in the center. In this Square, on the west side of Temple Street, are Trinity, Center, and North churches. Farther west is the old State House, built in the Grecian Doric style.

Yale College fronts this square on the west, occupying seventeen buildings, and its grounds comprise one-eighteenth part of the original town plot, including the birthplace of Gov. Elihu Yale, from whom it receives its name. He was not, however, its founder, (the Congregational Clergy of the State being entitled to that honor), but one of its most liberal patrons, and his name was adopted by the

TEMPLE STREET, NEW HAVEN.

College as a slight recognition of his munificence and labors in its behalf. Gov. Yale resided in New Haven many years, but afterward emigrated to the East Indies and became Governor of Fort George.

The College, which is one of the leading, if not

the best, educational institution in this country, was founded in 1700, and in 1702 it held its first commencement at Saybrook, but was removed to New Haven in 1716. The first College building stood near the corner of College and Chapel streets. The dates of the erection of the seventeen buildings at present occupied by the College, are as follows: South College was begun in 1793; the old Chapel, now the Athenæum, next north, in 1761; South Middle College in 1750; the Lyceum and North Middle in 1803; the Chapel in 1824; the North College in 1822; and Divinity College in 1835. This completes the list on College street. Those in the rear are: The old Dining Hall, now the Laboratory, in 1782; new Dining Hall, used as a Lecture Room below, and for a Mineralogical and Geological Cabinet above, in 1819; the Library in 1842; the Trumbull Gallery in 1831; Alumni Hall in 1852; Fine Arts Building in 1865-6; new Theological Building in 1868-9; Farnam Hall in 1869-70; Durfee Hall in 1870-1; and the Chapel of the Theological Department in 1871. The new Theological Building is 164 feet long, four stories high, and cost nearly $150,000. Farnam Hall was built from funds donated by Henry Farnam, of New Haven. Durfee Hall is the gift of Dr. Nathan Durfee, of Fall River, Mass., and cost upwards of $100,000. Both Farnam and Durfee Halls are used for apartments for the students. The Yale School of Fine Arts was founded by the late Augustus R. Street, of New Haven. It provides for the collection and exhibition of works of Art, and for instruction in the principles and theory of Art. The historical paintings of the great battles in the Revolution, by Col. John Trumbull, son of the Governor of Connecticut during the war for Independence, and an aid to Gen. Washington, are to be found in this building. These are the original paintings, and copies of them are now in the rotunda of the National Capitol. Alumni Hall, built of Portland freestone, at a cost of $27,000, is a fine structure. The first floor is occupied for the meetings of graduates, and around this room are hung portraits of distinguished men, educated in the College, and others who have contributed to its endowment. The upper story is used by the two College societies. The Library of Yale College is one of the best in the country, and now contains nearly 90,000 volumes. The building for the Sheffield Scientific School, which is very fine, is the gift of Joseph E. Sheffield, a wealthy citizen of New Haven.

A NUT FOR PHILOSOPHERS TO CRACK.

A New Haven gentleman, who has made student life and character a study, says that, after fifty years of careful observation, he has come to the conclusion that strict honor and integrity in the average student is in proportion to the distance that his home is situated from the College. If he lives in New Haven, you will find him generally honest. If he lives just outside of the city, he will prevaricate; fifty miles out, he tells white lies; one hundred miles, he doesn't hesitate to tell a lie when it serves his purpose; five hundred miles, lies when the truth would do a great deal better; one thousand miles and upward, can't be believed under oath. When interrogated as to what profession the different grades enter, after graduating, he produced the following table, compiled with great care and from reliable sources: Home in New Haven, or near the College, become divinity students and enter the ministry; fifty miles out, study medicine, and

write "M.D." after their names; 100 miles, become lawyers; 1000 miles and upward, if they fail to gain admission to the bar, they turn their attention to politics, or become independent journalists. Our informant is unable to account for this obtuseness of moral sentiment, unless it comes from the fact, that the students are required to attend prayers so early in the morning, that they spend most of their energies in framing plausible excuses for non-attendance, and in this way utterly lose their natural regard for the truth. It is possible that it may be explained on an entirely different theory.

PUBLIC BUILDINGS AND CELEBRATED MEN.

Of the public buildings, of which New Haven may feel proud, is the City Hall, situated on Church street, fronting the Square on the east. It was completed in 1862, at a cost of $100,000. The building is of the Continental Gothic style, 91 feet front by 137 feet deep. It was built of Portland and Nova Scotia stone, laid in alternate courses. The tower is built of stone, 84 feet from the ground, surmounted by a spire 66 feet high, making the total hight 150 feet. The spire is slated, and contains a fire-alarm bell weighing 6,117 pounds, four illuminated clock dials, each seven feet in diameter, and an observatory or watch tower. The building is occupied by offices, city court, common council chamber, &c.

There are nearly forty churches in the city, and the population is about 55,000. In 1800 the population was only a little over 5,000. A large variety of manufacturing is done in the city, but the most important is that of carriages. There are between forty and fifty firms engaged in the business.

Here have lived and died some of our country's most eminent men. In the cemetery on Grove street are the graves of Roger Sherman, one of the signers of the Declaration of Independence, Noah Webster, author of Webster's Dictionary, and other books, Ezra Stiles and Timothy Dwight, Presidents of Yale College, Pierpont Edwards, Chief Justice of Connecticut, James Hillhouse, for fifty years treasurer of Yale College, and sixteen years United States Senator, Chauncey A. Goodrich—" Peter Parley,"—Margaret Arnold, wife of the traitor, Benedict Arnold, Eli Whitney, inventor of the cotton gin, and many others more or less distinguished in various walks of life. Col. John Dixwell, one of the judges who condemned King Charles I, lived in New Haven, assuming the name of James Davids. He died at the age of eighty-two, and was buried in the rear of Center church, on the Public Square, where a monument has recently been erected to his memory by his descendants.

James Hillhouse, who, for so long a time, was treasurer of Yale College, and to whom New Haven is indebted for its noble elms, was very tall and commanding in personal appearance. His complexion was so swarthy that some thought he had Indian blood in his veins, and he frequently favored, in a humorous way, this idea. While a member of the United States Senate, a Southern man challenged him for remarks made in debate. The challenge was accepted, and, as the choice of weapons fell to him, he selected *tomahawks!* The duel was not fought. One day, while standing on the steps of the Capitol, a drove of donkeys were passing, on their way from Connecticut, where they were raised, to the South. Randolph, who was with him, said, "*there are some of your constituents.*" "Yes," replied Hillhouse, "they are going to be *schoolmasters* in Virginia."

New Haven formerly had considerable direct trade with foreign countries, and long wharf, commencing at the foot of Fleet street and extending into the harbor to the channel, 3,943 feet, is the longest wharf in this country.

THE NEW HAVEN HOTEL.

The New Haven Hotel, S. H. Moseley, Proprietor, is situated on the corner of Chapel and Church streets, within five minutes walk of the depot. It fronts on the Public Square, and, as it is provided with all the modern conveniences, bath rooms, &c., visitors will find it a pleasant place of resort, as it is one of the best kept hotels in the country.

RAILROAD CONNECTIONS.

The Railroads terminating at New Haven, are the Shore Line to New London and Providence; the Air Line to Middletown and Willimantic, the New Haven and Derby, to Derby; and the New Haven and Northampton. The latter extends from New Haven to Williamsburg, a distance of 84 miles connecting at Plainville with the Hartford, Providence and Fishkill; at Farmington with branch to Collinsville and New Hartford; at Simsbury with the Connecticut Western; at Westfield with the Boston and Albany, and branch to Ingleside and Holyoke; at Easthampton with a branch of the Connecticut River Railroad to Mt. Tom; at Northampton with the Connecticut River Railroad, and Massachusetts Central, now building. A through car is run on the express trains, twice a day, from the Grand Central Depot, in New York, to Williamsburg, enabling passengers to go through without change.

GOING NORTH.

Leaving the "City of Elms," the train passes under Chapel street, across the stone bridge over Mill River, past East Rock, which is on the left, and the broad salt meadows to the right, through the village of North Haven, immediately beyond which the scenery is of no particular interest, the surface of the country being level, and the soil light and sandy.

WALLINGFORD.—THE COMMUNITY.

Twelve miles from New Haven, east of the railroad, will be noticed the village of Wallingford, situated on a commanding eminence. Express trains do not stop here. Quite an extensive business is done in manufacturing plated ware, buttons, &c.

Lyman Hall, one of the signers of the Declaration of Independence, was a native of Wallingford. After graduating at Yale, he went to Georgia, where he established himself as a physician. Taking an active part in colonial affairs, he was chosen to the General Congress in 1775, and afterwards Governor of Georgia. He died in 1790, and was buried in his adopted State. Just previous to the rebellion, Georgia made Connecticut a present of his tombstones, and they were taken to Wallingford and deposited in the cemetery south of the depot.

Situated on the slope of "Mount Tom," an eminence three-fourths of a mile west of Wallingford Station, is a branch of the Oneida Community, in Central New York, with which it holds a common interest. The Wallingford Society was organized in 1851, with a capital of $5,500. Its present capital is much larger. The primary object of the Community, it is claimed, is the religious culture of its members in accordance with what they conceive to be the spirit and doctrines of the New Testament. They believe in the power of Christianity to save individuals from all sin, in consequence of which belief they are called Perfectionists. Their social system includes full Communion of property, or holding "all things in common," like that of the day of Pentecost. The domain comprises 228 acres, of which 30 are in orcharding and vineyards. A new building for publishing and educational purposes was erected in 1865, at a cost of $3,500. Several young men of the Community have been maintained as students in the legal and medical departments of Yale College.

THE HANGING HILLS.

The tourist, while near Wallingford, will observe the Hanging Hills, or Sentinels of the Valley, west of Meriden. These peaks, which seem to rise abruptly to considerable hight, are the most elevated points of land in the State, and are the first objects seen by sailors coming into Sandy Hook, below New York. A road has been constructed through a narrow glen in these hills, from Meriden to Berlin, known as Cat-Hole Pass, which is much frequented by summer tourists and neighboring residents.

MERIDEN.

Meriden, where express trains stop, is midway between New Haven and Hartford, it being just 18 miles to either place. It has a population of about 12,000 and is one of the most active and prosperous towns in the State. From 1850 to 1860 it showed a greater proportionate increase in population than any other town in Connecticut. There is little or no inherited wealth in the town, although the assessments now amount to six millions. Twenty years ago there was no one residing in the town who was worth $40,000. At the present time there are more than a dozen residents whose property is valued at from $100,000 to half a million each, while there are others who have accumulated large estates by their foresight and industry. Manufacuturing is the principal business of the town, there being fifty different establishments, and a large variety of goods are made here and sent to all parts of the country. The most extensive concern is that of the Meriden Britannia Company, whose factory stands east of the railroad and near the depot. The company manufacture a large variety of plated table ware. A large business is done in the town in manfacturing ivory piano keys, ivory combs, cutlery, door knobs, lamp trimmings, balmoral skirts, hardware, castings, &c. The old town, where the first settlement was made, is delightfully situated on the hill, east of the depot and the large square building, standing at the head of the street is the Town Hall. That part of the village on the hill is known as Meriden, and that at the depot and west of it, as West Meriden. Each village has a separate post office. There are nine churches in the town—three Congregational, two Baptist, an Episcopal, Methodist, Universalist, and Catholic. The State Reform School, a large brick building, will be noticed west of the railroad, and about a mile north of the depot.

MOUNT LAMENTATION.

East of Meriden is a range of mountains similar to the Hanging Hills on the west of the town, known as Mount Lamentation, a not very poetical name, but having its origin, it is said, in some sad local tradition.

Continuing north, the next stopping place for express trains is,

BERLIN JUNCTION.

The village of Berlin is situated on a hill east of the railroad, a little way south of the depot. From this place are two branch railroads, one extending north-west to New Britain, two and a half miles, and the other south-east, ten miles, to Middletown on the Connecticut.

NEW BRITAIN.

The church spires of the town can be seen from Berlin Junction. This is a thriving and enterprising place, with a population of 6,000 and is pleasantly situated. The principal business is that of manufacturing locks and builders' hardware, rules, levels, bolts, hinges, shirts and drawers, cabinet hardware, harness and saddlery hardware, hooks and eyes, sash fasteners and curtain fixtures. The manufacturing is all done by steam power and has thus far been successfully conducted. The village is supplied with water brought two and a half miles, from Shuttle Meadow Lake. The fountain on the Green is said to be the largest in the country and will throw a stream to the hight of 140 feet. The State Normal School is located here.

HARTFORD.

New York, 110; White Mountains, 218; Lake Memphremagog, 257; Montreal, 338; Quebec, 418 miles.

A RIDE of a few miles from Berlin Junction brings you within sight of the tall spires of Hartford. South of the depot and Asylum Street, is the Park, which was purchased by the city a few years since at a cost of over $270,000. It contains 30 acres. The grounds are neatly and tastefully laid out, and the whole alike creditable to the wisdom and liberality of the people of the city. Park River forms the northern boundary of the Park and is crossed by several stone bridges, and that at the junction of Ford and Pearl Streets, in sight of the depot, built of Portland freestone, is a beautiful structure. Hartford has a population of about 50,000. In 1800 it was only a little more than 5,000 and up to 1840 it had reached only a little over 12,000. Whitin the last ten or fifteen years new enterprises have sprung up and its growth has been quite rapid, and at the present time there are few places of its size that have so much substantial prosperity. Statistics show that it has more wealth in proportion to its inhabitants than any other city in this country. It has a large mercantile and manufacturing business, but it is chiefly known abroad on account of its numerous insurance companies. In this respect it is the leading city in the country. There are no less than nineteen insurance companies in operation, with a capital of $20,000,000, and all of them are doing a successful business. Of this number eleven are devoted to fire, six to life and one to accident insurance. The latter is the first of its kind in the country. Its moneyed institutions stand equally high in public estimation although confined to a more limited sphere of action. There are twelve banks of issue with a capital of $8,000,000, and four savings institutions.

In Colonial times, Hartford took a leading position, and then as well as now was a place of no small consequence. There are still many things in existence in the city that are of historical interest, especially to those having a taste for the rare and curious belonging to other days. No one passing through the city, with time at his command, should fail of spending a few days in visiting its many interesting localities. He could not go away without feeling doubly paid for his time and trouble. Although a severe gale in 1856 blew down the famous Charter Oak, pieces of it are preserved, and at the State House, in the office of the Secretary of State, is the identical charter, framed in the wood of the tree that once concealed it from Sir Edmund Andros.

the first Governor-general of New England, who in 1676 attempted to wrest it from the people of Connecticut. The demand for building lots has greatly changed the old Wyllys place, where the Charter Oak stood, situated east of Main Street, in the southern part of the city, but a marble slab at the side of the walk, in Charter Oak Place, has been placed over the spot where the old tree took root and spread its noble branches.

The old State House, which stands on Main street, was built in 1794. The State having made Hartford the sole capital, a new State House, that will cost at least three million dollars, is now in process of erection. The city purchased Trinity College buildings and part of its grounds just south of the Park, at a cost of $600,000, and donated this and $500,000 in addition, to the State, as its contribution. The old State House goes to the city and will be used for various city purposes. Trinity College has purchased grounds in the southern part of the city where buildings are being erected. In the State Library are preserved many letters from the kings of England during Colonial times to the Governors in Connecticut. The oldest one was written in 1666 and bears upon it the autograph of Charles II. In the Senate Chamber is the Governor's chair that was made of wood from the Charter Oak. It is handsomely carved and inlaid, and upon it is the State Coat of Arms. Here is a full length, original painting of Washington by Stewart. Here also hang the portraits of the governors, from John Winthrop of Colonial days to the present occupant of the gubernatorial chair. Oliver Wolcot, Sr., whose portrait is among the number, was one of the signers of the Declaration of Independence, and afterwards Secretary of the Treasury during Washington's and John Adams' administrations. In the south chamber of the old State House was held the famous Hartford Convention.

In the Historical Rooms in Wadsworth Athenæum, will be found some rare relics of olden times. Among them, Elder Wm. Brewster's chest, that came over with him in the Mayflower; Miles Standish's dinner pot; Benedict Arnold's watch; Gen. Israel Putnam's tavern sign, and the sword carried by him at Bunker Hill; a link of the chain stretched across the Hudson at West Point, in the Revolution; bombshells that were thrown into Stonington during the last war; an arm chair made in the 13th century; the vest and shirt of Col. Ledyard, commander of Fort Griswold when surrendered to the British Sept. 6, 1781, and who was massacred after the surrender; Nathan Hale's powder horn, made by him during his college vacations; a mortar captured at the city of Mexico; the first telegraph message sent in this country, between Washington and Baltimore; an old drum used at Farmington to call the people to church; Dr. Robbin's collection of Bibles, one of them printed in 1478.

But of all the rare and curious things found here, none are of more interest by way of showing the rapid developement of the country, than the little six by nine mail bag used in 1775, to carry the mail between Hartford, Middletown and New Haven.

The first settlement made in Hartford was by the Dutch in 1633, who landed on the point of land at the junction of park River with the Connecticut, where they built a Fort. One of the bricks used in its construction is now in the Historical Rooms. This place is still known as Dutch Point. The first English settlement was made in 1635, the settlers coming from Cambridge, Mass. The first meeting house in Connecticut was built at Hartford in 1638, and some of its timbers are said to have been used in the construction of the present Center Congregational Church. Thomas Green established the Connecticut Courant in October, 1764, the first paper and printing office in Hartford, and John I. Wells received in 1819 a patent for the first lever printing press. Dr. A. Kinsley, invented the first steam engine ever made, in 1797-9, and set it running in Main Street. He also invented the first brick pressing machine. The "Mansion House," on Kinsley Street, built in 1796 is probably the oldest house in this country, built of pressed bricks that were made here.

Main Street, one of the finest in any New England city, extending north and south, is two miles in length. The retail trade is principally done here. State Street, extending east from Main Street to the River is occupied by those doing a wholesale business in groceries, dye stuffs, wool, tobacco, leather and iron. Hartford is one of the largest markets for wool and tobacco of any city in New England. An extensive wholesale trade is done on Asylum Street in dry goods.

The factory built by Col. Samuel Colt, for the manufacture of his celebrated revolvers was one of the largest enterprises ever undertaken. Since Col. Colt's death it has been conducted by a company, of which Brig. Gen. Franklin is now president. Employment is given to eight hundred hands. The front building was burnt in 1864, but it was rebuilt in 1866. The establishment is situated in the southeast part of the city, near the Connecticut, and is inclosed by a dyke, fifty feet broad at the top and 8,698 feet in length. It incloses 23 acres of land, and cost over $80,000. Col. Colt assumed the responsibility and built the dyke at his own expense, but the city afterward paid part of the cost. Few men had so determined a purpose, and were so hard to be swerved from their line of policy as Col. Colt. Starting as a poor boy, he worked his way to fame and wealth, and when he died he left an immense fortune to his wife and young son. His dwelling, grounds, and extensive green house on Wethersfield Avenue, which overlook the Armory, built by himself, surpass anything in the city. Within the dyke inclosure is a colony of Swiss, brought to this country by Col. Colt to manufacture willow ware, the material for which is grown along the dyke.

The Weed Sewing Machine, one of the best of the first-class machines, is made here. S. L. Clark, the Secretary of the Company, is the active manager.

Of the public institutions may be mentioned the Wadsworth Athenæum, Trinity College, The Connecticut Theological Institute, Deaf and Dumb Asylum, Retreat for the Insane, and Hartford Hospital. The Athenæum, was erected by contributions from citizens of Hartford, at a cost of $52,000. It was constructed of granite and is 80 by 100 feet. In this building are the Connecticut Historical Rooms, Young Men's Institute, and the Watkinson Library. Also rooms devoted to paintings and statuary. The Watkinson Library is one of reference and no book can be taken from it except on the written consent of the trustees. It was founded by David Watkinson, who died Dec. 13, 1857, aged 80 years, leaving $100,000 for the purpose of establishing the Library. Rare works were purchased in Europe, and the library was first opened to the public in the early part of 1866. The Young Men's Institute contains 13,000 volumes which can be taken from the rooms. The Deaf and Dumb Asylum, located on Asylum Street, west of the depot, is the oldest institution of its kind in this country, having been incorporated in 1816. The late Rev. T. H. Gallaudet, LL.D. visited Europe for the purpose of ascertaining the best method of imparting instruction to the deaf and dumb, and brought with him on his return M. Laurent Clerc, a deaf mute who had been a successful teacher in Paris, and who acted as an assistant to Mr. Gallaudet. It was opened with seven deaf mutes as pupils, and the number has since been increased to 275. The main building was erected in 1850 and is 130 by 50 feet, four stories high. The Retreat for the Insane was opened in 1824. It is situated in the southern part of the city, on Washington Street, on a gentle elevation commanding an extensive view of the city, the river and the valley beyond. The grounds contain 17 acres and are tastefully ornamented with walks and shade trees. During the 50 years of its existence there have been admitted to it over 4,000 patients, more than half of whom were discharged as cured. The Hartford Hospital was opened in 1859. The main building is 72 by 42 feet, three stories high, with a wing 113 by 30 feet. It is built of Portland stone, and cost, including grounds, over $48,000. Any persons paying $1,000 at one time will be entitled to a free bed.

The city is supplied with water from the Connecticut River, and from Trout Brook, five miles west of the city. The fall from Trout Brook to foot of State Street is 210 feet.

The repair shops of New Haven, Hartford and Springfield Railroad, are located at this place, a short distance south of the depot. The passenger depot, occupied jointly by the New Haven, Hartford and Springfield and Providence, Hartford and Fishkill Railroads, at this place, is one of the finest in the country. It was built of Portland freestone, and is a large and substantial building.

Hartford has several hotels, the largest and most elegant of which is the Allyn House, situated at the corner of Asylum and Trumbull Streets. It was erected in 1857 at a cost of $125,000. It is four stories high, with a front of 155 feet on Asylum Street, and 105 on Trumbull. The front is built of Portland stone and altogether is not surpassed by any hotel in New England. The first floor of the building is occupied by stores, and the remainder

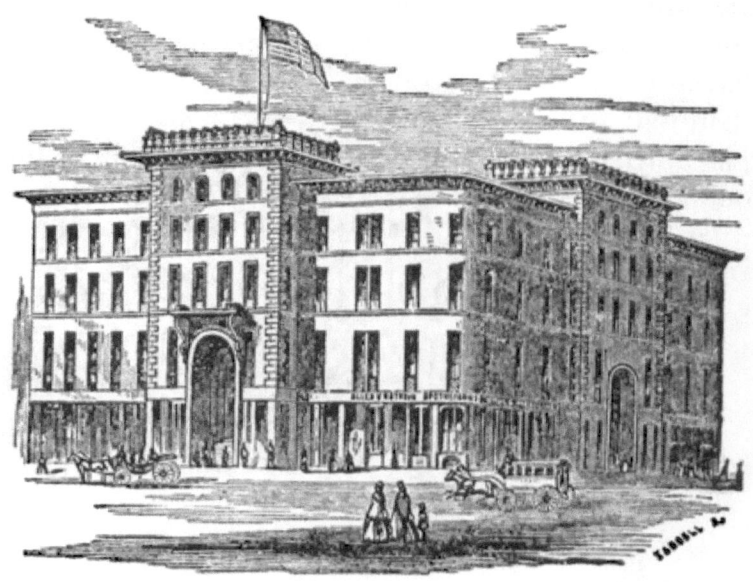

ALLYN HOUSE, HARTFORD, CONN.

is used for hotel purposes. There are accommodations for nearly 300 guests. Everything connected with it is neatly and conveniently arranged, and no pains have been spared to make this a first class hotel in every respect. The proprietor, Mr. R. J. Allyn, is courteous and obliging, and makes the stranger at once feel at home. Adjoining the Allyn

House, on the west, and connected with it by a private entrance, is Allyn Hall, one of the largest and finest in Connecticut. It will seat 1,500 people.

The streets of the city are McAdamized, and the drives through and about it are unsurpassed. Among them may be mentioned,—to Tumble Down Brook, eight miles west by Albany road; to Talcott Mountain, nine miles west; to West Hartford, three and a half miles; to Wethersfield, four miles; to Glastenbury, four miles; over Newington Mountain, three and one half miles; to Prospect Hill; to Bloomfield, and to Shipman's at Rocky Hill, some seven miles.

Hartford has good railroad facilities. Besides the New York, New Haven and Hartford, extending to Springfield, it has the Providence and Fishkill, the Connecticut Western, and the Connecticut Valley, the latter extending from Hartford to Saybrook on the Sound, at the mouth of the Connecticut River.

WINDSOR.

The first English settlement in Connecticut was made at Windsor in 1633. William Holmes and others erected a house on Farmington River, near its mouth, and the land in its vicinity is still known as Plymouth Meadow. The Dutch Governor at New York sent a force to assault the house erected by Holmes, and drive the English away, but it was so well fortified that the exepdition returned without doing it, after making friends with the English. Roger Wolcott, Governor of Connecticut from 1751 to

1754, and Oliver Ellsworth, Senator and Chief Justice of the United States, were born in this town. Windsor is a pleasant country village, but is not a place of much business.

SOUTH WINDSOR.

South Windsor, situated on the east side of the Connecticut, and six miles north of Hartford, is distinguished as being the birthplace of Jonathan Edwards, the great American divine, John Fitch, the inventor of the steam boat, and Oliver Wolcott, one of the signers of the Declaration of Independence, and the Governor of Connecticut in 1796. During the Revolutionary war many prisoners were sent here for safe keeping, and among them were William Franklin, the royal governor of New Jersey, and son of Dr. Franklin, Gen. Hamilton and Gen. Prescott. Gov. Franklin was quartered at the house of Lieut. Diggin, about a mile south of the Congregational church, where with his servants, he lived in princely style. He was extremely fond of sour punch, and in a bower situated in a retired spot, back of the street, near Podunk Brook, he prepared and served his favorite beverage to the French visitors, who styled it "one grand contradiction." South Windsor was the headquarters of Gen. LaFayette, in 1788, after the project of invading Canada was abandoned, and he remained at the house of Mr. Porter during his stay in town, about three-quarters of a mile south of the Congregational church, which was provided for defense by portholes for muskets. Many of the elm trees now standing were set out by the British and Hessian prisoners at the suggestion of Gen. LaFayette, who held one end of the line while Mr. Porter held the other. The trees were planted in rows parallel with the street. While LaFayette resided here he was visited by Washington, and in order to do honor to the occasion he requested Lieut. King to appear with a company of mounted men. Forty-two men were mustered, equipped somewhat ludicrously with sheep skins for saddles and canes for swords, and LaFayette introduced them as follows: "Gen. Washington, I presume you are acquainted with this troop." The General replied, "I do not remember that I ever before had the honor of seeing them." Much to Washington's amusement, LaFayette expressed his surprise, remarking, that they had seen much service and were known as the "Old Testament Guard."

THE STONE BRIDGE, NEAR WINDSOR.

North of Windsor station the railroad company have built across Farmington River a substantial stone bridge, 450 feet in length, with seven arches, at a cost of $40,000.

WINDSOR LOCKS.

A few miles further north, on the banks of the Connecticut is the manufacturing village of Windsor Locks. The water power is furnished from a canal on the west side of the river, five miles in length, that was built many years ago, around Enfield Falls, for the purpose of improving the Connecticut. Sloops and small steamboats, laden with merchandise, going to towns higher up the Connecticut, used to pass through the canal and thence around the rapids in the river. Since the construction of the railroad, this canal has become of no use so far as its original purpose is concerned, but the ingenuity of man has seized upon it and compelled it to contribute to his material wants. Considerable manufacturing is done here.

THE GREAT IRON BRIDGE ACROSS THE CONNECTICUT AT WAREHOUSE POINT.

Passing Windsor Locks, you come to one of the finest bridges in this country—the great Iorn Truss Bridge across the Connecticut at Warehouse Point, midway between Hartford and Springfield. It is 1,525 feet long, weighs, including the track and floor beams, upon which the track rests, about 800 tons, and cost $265,000. The chief engineer of this noble structure was Mr. James Laurie, a Scotchman by birth, who, for several years, was President of the board of Civil Engineers in this country, and for a time at the head of the Government engineers in Nova Scotia. He was assisted by Theo. G. Ellis, Engineer of Hartford Dyke. The plans were made in 1862 and submitted to a Philadelphia firm, but owing to the great demands upon American iron workers, for Government work, for war purposes, it could not be built in this country as soon as required. After some delay, it was decided to have the bridge built in England, and in January, 1864, Mr. Laurie sailed for Europe to give out the contracts. On arriving in England he proceeded to

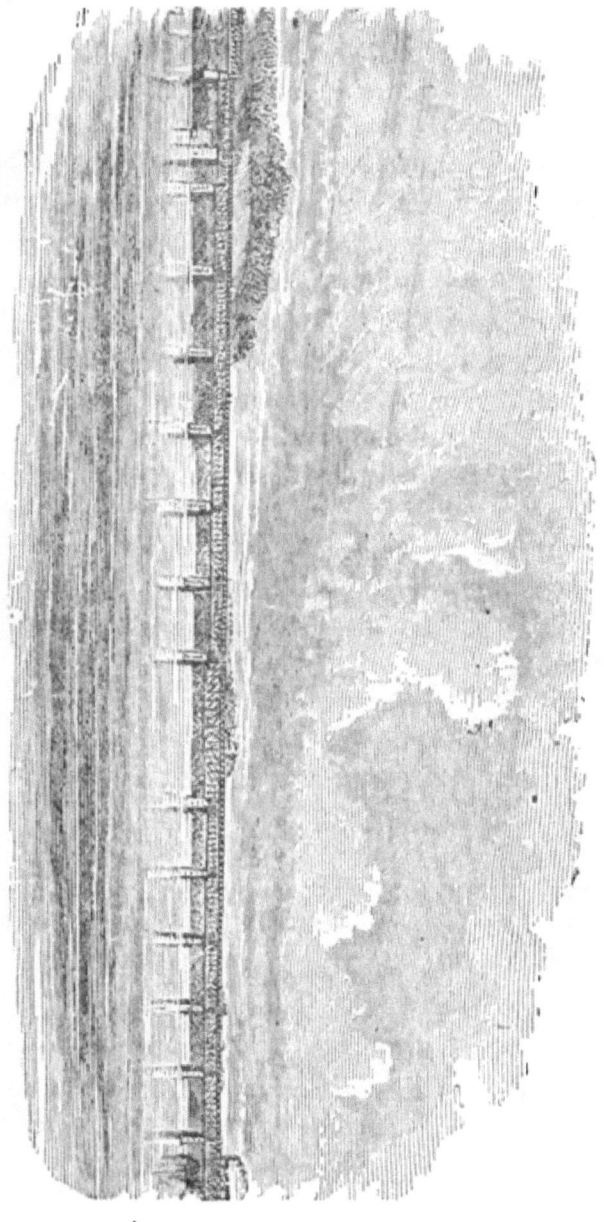

THE GREAT IRON BRIDGE OVER THE CONNECTICUT AT WAREHOUSE POINT.

Manchester where he contracted with William Fairbairn & Sons, they agreeing to make the iron for the bridge by the first of December. Subsequently, it appearing that they would not be able to finish the work as soon as specified, part of it was given to the London Engineering and Iron Ship Building Company. In about a year the bridge was shipped from Liverpool and London, and in June, 1865, work upon its erection begun. About one hundred workmen, many of whom came specially from England, were employed, and in Feb. 1866 it was completed. There are seventeen spans in the bridge, the longest of which, the channel span, in the center of the river, is 177 1-3 feet. Eight of the other spans are 88 1-2 feet each, another is 140 feet, another 76 3-4 feet, another 43 feet, and another 25 1-2 feet, making the exact total length of the bridge 1,524 1-2 feet. Each span consists of a wrought iron truss, composed of horizontal plates, angle and T iron. The width of the deck of the bridge upon which the track rests is 17 3-4 feet; of the iron truss, canal span, 16 feet, of the channel span, 12 2-3 feet and of the others, 10 1-3 feet. The hight of the truss—channel span, 16 2-3 feet, canal span 12 1-3 feet, and of the others 11 feet. The horizontal plates in the four chords are from 15 to 25 feet in length, from one-fourth to three-fourths of an inch in thickness, and about eight inches in width. At the joints a short plate is riveted to each side of the main plate, and is so arranged that no two joints meet in the same place.

The plates and angle iron, which are riveted together, give each chord a trough-like shape. From the upper to the lower chord on each side of the bridge are iron posts, made of plate, angle and T iron. Across the posts on an angle of 45 degrees, extending from the bottom to the top chord on each side of the bridge, are bars of a few inches in width. In the short span these bars cross but one post to which they are firmly riveted, in the next longer two posts, and in the channel span three. The posts being several feet apart, from five to five and three-fourths feet, they give a lattice-like appearance to the bridge. Extending through the truss are lateral and vertical tie bars which help support it. The spans are securely fastened to the piers below. One end of each span rests upon four iron rollers which turn upon an iron bed-plate, and between the ends of the span is a space of an inch and a half, allowed for expansion. These rollers are upon every other pier—the end of the spans upon the intervening ones are firmly secured to the masonry, so there can be no possibility of the bridge getting out of place. The frame of the bridge was all put together in England before shipping, and then part of it taken down. This was done to detect any mistake that might have occurred. There are 175,-000 rivets, from three-fourths to one and one-eighth inches in diameter, in the bridge. Part of them were put in by machinery in England, and the remainder by hand while the bridge was being erected. The piers of the old bridge, which are of Monson granite, were used, after raising them to a greater hight, and new ones were built between the old, doubling the number. To build the bridge and maintain the old one so as not to delay the trains, while the work was in progress, was an undertaking of no small magnitude. It was however accomplished, and of the 22 to 28 trains that cross the bridge daily, not a detention of a single minute was caused to them. The lower chords of the iron bridge were placed upon blocking, two feet in thickness, which rested upon the piers, and during Sunday, when there were no trains to pass, the completed span was lowered to its place by means of hydraulic jacks. The weight of the bridge, not including track and floor beams, is 624 tons, and its cost in England, in gold, was $85.58 per ton. In New York, in currency, its cost was $241.54 per ton. The freight from London and Liverpool to New York, was $3.75 per ton. Some of the other items of cost are as follows: Freight from London and Liverpool to New York, $2,342.10; duty, $30.12 per ton; making a total of $18,796.40; paid premium on gold, $73,120.68; cost of bridge in England, $53,400.22; cost of iron work, erected, $173,109.-62; cost of labor for erection, including tools, $16,-985.34; cost of masonry, $15,744.07. It will be seen by this that the premium on gold, which was then in the vicinity of 100, amounted to $19,720.46 more than the cost of the bridge in England, when ready for shipment. The track passes over the top of the bridge, excepting the span over the canal, and the view up and down the river is very fine. The distance from the top of the rails to low water mark is 47 feet. This is the most extensive iron bridge in the United States, but for several years, the New York Central, Baltimore and and Ohio, Pennsylvania Central Railroads have tested them, on a smaller scale, and have become satisfied of their durability. It is thought that this bridge will last a century. The strength of the bridge must be very great, and it is estimated that a continuous line of locomotives, from one shore to the other, would not exceed more than one-seventh of the weight it is capable of sustaining. During the construction of the bridge no serious accident occurred. One workman fell through a thirteen inch hole into the river, a distance of forty feet, and struck in water that was only nine inches deep. He was disabled only for a few days, and then continued work until the bridge was completed. Two wooden bridges have been built in this place—the first one in 1844, when the road was opened. It was blown down in October, 1846, and rebuilt in forty-five days.

WAREHOUSE POINT.

Crossing the Connecticut on the iron bridge you come to Warehouse Point, a way station at the east end of the bridge on the bank of the river. Formerly this was a place of some note, it being the head of sloop navigation. The place received its name from the fact that warehouses for the storage of merchandise were located here. The boats unloaded at this place, and there cargoes were transferred to wagons and carried to the several towns farther up the Connecticut.

ENFIELD.—HAZARD POWDER WORKS.—THE SHAKERS.

Passing Warehouse Point, the village of Enfield will be noticed on the hill to the east. This is a quiet, rural town, overlooking the Connecticut and the valley for many miles. The northern limits of the town extend to the boundary line between Connecticut and Massachusetts. Four miles east of the river is Hazardville, where are located part of the powder mills that were owned by the late Col. A. G. Hazard. During the Rebellion he furnished a large quantity of powder for the Government, and England, during the Crimean war, purchased a million and a quarter dollars, worth of him. There are no powder works in England so large as these. The powder is taken to the magazine, near Enfield station, and from there sent down the river in small boats. Col. Hazard was for thirty years engaged in the manufacture of powder, and acquired a large property. His acquaintance with the public men of the country was extensive, and when Webster was at the zenith of his fame, he was among his personal friends. Gov. A. H. Bullock of Massachusetts married one of his daughters.

The Shakers have one of their largest communities in this town, six miles east of the river. They number several hundred members, and are a very industrious and thriving people.

Suffield, one of the best farming towns in Connecticut, is on the west side of the river. The village is reached by cars from Windsor Locks. It cannot be seen from the cars, but this brings us to

A HORSE STORY.

Mr. O., of Enfield, liked nothing better than a good horse, and Mr. A., of Suffield, was equally pleased with a good bargain. He bought a venerable animal, and by liberal feeding, added largely to his good appearance. Meeting Mr. O., he invited him over to see his fast horse—"a leetle the fastest nag ever seen in town." The day was named and he went over. Just before he reached Mr. A.'s house, an application of turpentine and pepper was made to the animal's tail. By instructions, the wife and daughter were to appear at the door and object to the sale of the horse. Soon after Mr. O. appeared. The horse was brought out, and, smarting from the turpentine application he had received, plunged about, and altogether, was the most mettlesome animal to be found in town. The wife and daughter came out of doors, the latter exclaiming, "Oh, father! don't sell that horse! You shan't sell it! Don't you know how I drove him to Feeding Hills, and what a nice time I had?" This reassured Mr. O., and, on the whole, he thought that was just the horse he had been looking after. He inquired the price, pulled out his pocketbook, and paid for the horse. He drove him home, and a livelier animal he had never owned. He was put into the stable, that night, with no small degree of satisfaction; but the next morning, when he was harnessed for a ride, Mr. O. found the horse quite a different animal. He was stiff and broken down. In fact, he could not be pounded out of a walk. Taking in the situation, after he had carefully looked over the animal, he started for Suffield, and, after a good deal of labor, succeeded in getting back with the

"JUST THE HORSE I WANT."

horse to Mr. A.'s house. He entered the house and inquired for the young lady. "Miss A., did you say that you drove that horse to Feeding Hills?" "Yes," replied the young lady; "and I had a nice time, too." "Did you swear any?" "*Swear!* what do you mean?" "Didn't you get mad?" "Certainly not. What do you mean?" "Well, all I have to say, is, that if you drove *that* horse to Feeding Hills, and didn't swear, and didn't get mad, you are fit for the kingdom of Heaven!" Mr. O.

"THIS IS THE HORSE I GOT."

returned home, and that is the last horse he has bought in Suffield.

THOMPSONVILLE.—THE HARTFORD CARPET WORKS.

Two miles north of Enfield bridge, and in the town of Enfield, is the manufacturing village of Thompsonville, named in honor of Col. Orrin Thompson, the founder of the Hartford Carpet Works, located at this place. The manufacture of carpets was begun in 1828, and this establishment is now one of the largest of its kind in the country. The varieties made are Ingrain and Venetian, and the quality is said to be superior to anything found in the American market, and so much so that foreign Ingrain carpets, have been superseded by them. The machinery, at these mills, is driven entirely by steam, three engines, one of them 500 horse power, being used for that purpose. The consumption of coal in a single year, amounts to 3000 tons. There are in the mills 127 Ingrain and 14 Venetian power looms, and there are manufactured daily 6000 yards of Ingrain carpeting. The wool consumed is all imported, as there are no breeds of sheep in this country, producing a quality sufficiently coarse, to be used in manufacturing carpets. It requires 6000 pounds of wool per day, to keep the mills in full operation. The capital of the Company is $1,500,000.

LONGMEADOW.

Within four miles of Springfield, on the plateau, east of the railroad, will be noticed the village of Longmeadow. The boundary line between Massachusetts and Connecticut crosses the Connecticut River between this place and Thompsonville. Longmeadow was settled in 1644, eight years after the settlement of Springfield. It is one of those quiet rural towns, with large beautiful elms, so common in New England.

SPRINGFIELD.

New York, 135; White Mountains, 184; Lake Memphremagog, 229; Montreal, 310; Quebec, 390 miles.

APPROACHING Springfield from the south, as the train passes around the bend in the river, the city will be noticed on the left, and then again on the right, spread out over the hillside, more than a mile distant. The illustration on the next page is an excellent representation, and gives a correct impression of the general appearance of the city from this approach. The most prominent buildings to be seen are the United States Arsenal, on Armory Square, and St. Michael's (Catholic) Church, west and below it. The city contains 30,000 inhabitants, and is rapidly increasing in wealth and importance. It is compactly built for a provincial city, and numbers among its inhabitants some of the most enterprising people in New England. In a comparative sense, Springfield has not been so much distinguished for its manufactories as for being a great natural commercial center. A few years ago, with few exceptions, very little manufacturing was done within what are now the limits of the city; but more re-

cently the manufacturing interests have been greatly increased. Here center long lines of railways, from north, south, east, and west, with direct communication with all the large cities of the country, while for nearly fifty miles on either line, out of Springfield, and contributory to its trade and business, are large and thriving towns.

The United States Armory, which was established here in 1795, has probably been the chief source of prosperity to the town, although the number of hands employed, previous to the Rebellion, seldom exceeded 400. After the destruction of the Harper's Ferry Armory, early in the war, a large force, at one time 3,200 men, were kept at work, divided into two sets—one party working at night, and another during the day. There were manufactured during the four years of the Rebellion, from April, 1861, to June 30, 1865, 791,134 guns of various patterns, nearly all of which were borne over many a bloody battle field in defense of free institutions. This is a larger number of muskets than was manufactured during the first 65 years of the existence of the Armory, up to the commencement of the Rebellion. The amount of disbursements in 1865, that passed through the paymaster's hands, (Maj. Edward Ingersoll), including money and material used at the Armory, was $4,677,422, and for the whole time during the war, $12,000,000. The two squares on the hill, owned by the Government, comprise more than 72 acres. The Arsenal and the shops in which the muskets are made, excepting the welding of the barrels, are located on the western square, overlooking the city and the valley beyond. It is inclosed by an iron fence nine feet high, and the grounds are neatly and tastefully laid out. The view from the top of the Arsenal is particularly fine, exceeding, in some respects, that obtained from any other point in the city. The Arsenal, which is three stories high, will hold three hundred thousand muskets, and they are so regularly and neatly arranged in columns that they make a striking display. Some years ago Longfellow, after visiting the place, previous to the Rebellion, wrote the following lines, which were so prophetic and so expressive in the portrayal of the evils of war and bloodshed, that they will be read with renewed interest by every one who has been at the Arsenal:

THE ARSENAL AT SPRINGFIELD.

This is the Arsenal. From floor to ceiling,
    Like a huge organ, rise the burnished arms;
But from their silent pipes no anthem pealing
    Startles the villages with strange alarms.

Ah! what a sound will rise—how wild and dreary—
    When the death-angel touches those swift keys!
What loud lament and dismal Miserere
    Will mingle with their awful symphonies!

I here even now the infinite, fierce chorus—
    The cries of agony, the endless groan,
Which, through the ages that have gone before us,
    In long reverberations reach our own.

On helm and harness rings the Saxon hammer
    Through Cimbric forest roars the Norseman's song;

And loud, amid the universal clamor,
   O'er distant deserts sounds the Tartar gong.

I hear the Florentine, who from his palace
   Wheels out his battle-bell with dreadful din,
And Aztec priests upon their teocallis
   Beat the wild war-drums made of serpent's skin.

The tumult of each sacked and burning village;
   The shout that every prayer for mercy drowns;
The soldiers' revels in the midst of pillage,
   The wail of famine in beleaguered towns;

The bursting shell, the gateway wrenched asunder,
   The rattling musketry, the clashing blade—
And ever and anon, in tones of thunder,
   The diapason of the cannonade.

Is it, O man, with such discordant noises,
   With such accursed instruments as these,
Thou drownest Nature's sweet and kindly voices,
   And jarrest the celestial harmonies?

Were half the power that fills the world with terror,
   Were half the wealth bestowed on camps and courts
Given to redeem the human mind from error,
   There were no need of arsenals nor forts;

The warrior's name would be a name abhorred;
   And every nation that should lift again
Its hand against a brother, on its forehead
   Would wear forevermore the curse of Cain!

Down the dark future, through long generations,
   The echoing sounds grow fainter and then cease;
And like a bell, with solemn, sweet vibrations,
   I hear once more the voice of Christ say "Peace!"

Peace!—and no longer from its brazen portals,
   The blast of war's great organ shakes the skies;
But beautiful as songs of the immortals,
   The holy melodies of love arise.

The Water-Shops, located about a mile south east of the Arsenal, are particularly well adapted to the purposes for which they were constructed. Here all the barrels are made and tested.

Springfield cannot boast of so many pleasant drives as some of the other towns in its vicinity, but it has a few charming views. That from Long Hill, in the south part of the city, is as grand as it is extensive. The city on the right, the winding river on the left, the broad valley, checkered with a thousand fields, and the towering mountain peaks skirting the western horizon, present a beautiful and picturesque scene.

The cemetery, the principal entrance to which is from Maple Street, has few equals in natural beauty, or artificial adornment, when Mount Auburn and Greenwood are excepted. Inroads have been made upon Puritanical ideas even here, in the heart of New England, and the last resting places of the dead are now adorned by loving hands, stripping them of the more forbidding aspects that once distinguished them. No one should fail of spending a few hours, at least, in this secluded and beautiful spot.

Hampden Park, in the north part of the city, lying between the Connecticut River Railroad and the river, is conveniently situated and comprises a large number of acres. Here have been held several National Horse Shows and the County Agricultural Fairs. There are no better show grounds in New England. It is now used mostly as a trotting park, having been hired of the Agricultural Society by the Hampden Park Association.

Springfield is the oldest town in Massachusetts on the Connecticut River, having been settled in 1636, by a colony from Roxbury, and many of the descendants still live in the vicinity. The two principal business streets are Main and State—the former running parallel with the river, and the latter crossing it at right angles, extending from the Connecticut eastward, past the United States Armory. Many large and magnificent blocks have been erected on Main Street, within the last few years. During the war, owing to the large number of workmen employed at the armory, few towns were so prosperous.

The railroads terminating here are the New York, New Haven and Hartford, the Connecticut River, and the Springfield, Athol and Northeastern. The Boston and Albany Railroad crosses the Connecticut at this place on a substantial double-track iron bridge.

Here are located the repair shops of the Boston and Albany, and Connecticut River Railroads, giving employment to a large number of hands.

Of the several manufacturing establishments, the largest and most important are the Wason Manufacturing Company, and the Smith & Wesson. The former manufacture railroad cars of all descriptions, including passenger, sleeping, freight, coal, and horse railway cars, and the latter the celebrated Smith & Wesson pistol.

No hotel in New England, has acquired so extensive and deservedly good reputation, as the Massasoit House, and very few in the country are better known, and none are better kept. It is the pride of its proprietors, the boast of every Massachusetts man abroad, and the haven of rest, to the weary

THE MASSASOIT HOUSE, SPRINGFIELD, MASS.

and dusty traveler. The experience of hotel life is incomplete to all, who have not passed its portals. It is located close to the depot, and ample time is given to the tourist, for meals. The proprietors,

M. & E. S. Chapin, have long been engaged in the hotel business,—landlords of the Massasoit.

A raw-boned specimen of humanity, fresh from his native heath, came into the city one day, and meeting a boot black, near the Massasoit House, requested a "shine." Our street Arab, though he gen-

"HERE, BOY! BLACK 'THEM' BOOTS!"

really had an eye for business, was slightly astonished when he looked upon the size of his customer's boots. A happy thought, however, struck him as he took in the bearings of the case, and he delivered himself of the following: "Boots blacked! Number 9's! Mister, you just wait here a minute, till I go across the street and borrow five cents worth of spit."

COOLEY'S HOTEL.

Near the depot, just north of the railroad, is Cooley's Hotel. This house was opened in 1850, by J. M. Cooley, and is still kept by him. It is widely known, and there are no better managed hotels, in the country, than this. It has become so popular, that Mr. Cooley has been obliged to en-

COOLEY'S HOTEL, SPRINGFIELD, MASS.

large it, three separate times, since he first opened it. Here will be found good rooms, good attendance, and a well supplied table. Price, per day, $3.

THE WEST SPRINGFIELD CHURCH.—ANECDOTE OF DR. LATHROP.

Leaving Springfield for the north, the West Springfield Church, standing on a high bluff, on the west bank of the river, will be noticed. This church is seen for many miles up and down the valley. Here have preached more Doctors of Divinity than at any other country church, in New England, and some of them have been quite distinguished. Among them were Rev. Dr. Joseph Lathrop, Rev. Dr. Wm. B. Sprague, of Albany, and Rev. Dr. Thomas E. Vermilye, of New York. Rev. Henry M. Field, of New York, Editor of the Evangelist, son of Rev. Dr. Field, of Stockbridge, preached here for several years. Dr. Lathrop, it is said, was one of the most remarkable divines, that ever lived in the Connecticut valley, and during his ministry of 65 years, he wrote five thousand sermons, seven octavo volumes of which, have been published. An anecdote is related of him, which is said to be a good illustration of his character. A parishioner, for some trivial reason, had become very angry with him. Meeting him one day, he said, "Doctor, have you any religion?" "*None to boast of*," was the laconic reply.

BRIGHTWOOD.—THE WASON CAR WORKS.

Two miles north of Springfield, west of the railroad, are the car works of the Wason Manufacturing Company, located at what is now known as Brightwood, named in honor of Dr. J. G. Holland, who gave this name to his former beautiful home, upon the eminence to the east, now owned by Geo. C. Fisk, President of the Car Company. This Company has been one of the most successful in the country. Their shops were built in 1873, and are complete in every department. Some very beautiful cars are manufactured here, which are found upon the best roads in the United States and Canada. The business was commenced in 1845, by T. W. & C. Wason. The latter withdrew, in 1851, and in 1853, Geo. C. Fisk, L. O. Hanson and Josiah Bumstead were admitted as partners. In 1863, the firm procured an act of incorporation, and is now known as the Wason Manufacturing Company. Mr. Hanson and Mr. Bumstead subsequently withdrew, and after the death of T. W. Wason, in 1870, Mr. Fisk became President and General Manager of the concern. The Company have built cars for nearly 250 railroads, and their yearly business reaches about a million and a half dollars.

CHICOPEE.

Nearly four miles north of Springfield, is the manufacturing town of Chicopee, situated on the south bank of Chicopee River. The Dwight Manufacturing Company's Mills, seven in number, will be seen on the Chicopee River, nearest the railroad. The Ames Manufacturing Company, whose buildings can be seen east of the tall chimney, manufacture gun-stocking machinery, water wheels, bronze cannon, swords, bronze statuary, silver and plated ware. They are the largest manufacturers of bronze cannon in the country, and during the war, made over a thousand cannon, for the Government, besides a large quantity of shot and shell, running their works night and day, for three years, and employing 600 to 700 hands. In every gunboat, and on every battlefield, their cannon played a prominent part, in overcoming treason.

INGLESIDE HOTEL, NEAR HOLYOKE, MASS.

INGLESIDE.

Soon after leaving Chicopee, across the Connecticut, upon the hillside to the West, will be seen Ingleside Hotel, built by J. S. Davis, for a long time agent of the Lyman Mills at Holyoke, and now owned by N. S. Chandler. There is no more beautiful spot in the Connecticut Valley, and the view from the broad piazzas of the hotel is charming. The river below, the meadows beyond, and the more distant woodlands, which skirt the eastern hills, combined, make one of the most beautiful landscapes that can be found. The Hotel is two and a-half miles below Holyoke, and six and a-half from Springfield. The Holyoke and Westfield trains of the New Haven and Northampton Railroad stop in front of the Hotel. Mr. Chandler, the present proprietor, is a thorough landlord, and will make this one of the most attractive places of summer resort in New England, and the tourist will find it a delightful place to stop at. The hotel is well arranged, and contains all the latest improvements. A good farm is connected with the establishment, which supplies the hotel with fresh vegetables. Carriages are run from Holyoke to Ingleside, on the arrival of passengers.

This beautiful hotel was built at a cost of $162,000, but, during the year following the panic, it was sold at public auction to Mr. Chandler for a little less than $30,000. Mr. Chandler attended the sale with no expectation of purchasing, but, although the terms were exacting—$2,000 within half an hour after the sale, and the balance within five days—he was able to comply with them. He was afterward somewhat surprised to find that his purchase included fifteen acres of land on the east side of the Connecticut.

WILLIMANSETT.

This station is four miles from Chicopee. A few rods to the north the railroad crosses the Connecticut on a bridge 700 feet in length.

HOLYOKE.

Shortly before reaching Willimansett, the factories and public and private buildings of Holyoke are seen in the north-west. Here, eight miles from Springfield, is the greatest water power in New England, and here, at some future day, will be one of the largest manufacturing cities in America. Just north of the town, a dam, 30 feet high, and 1,017 feet in length, is built across the Connecticut. The river, at this point, falls 60 feet in a mile and a-half, and furnishes power sufficient to drive more than a million of cotton spindles—three times greater than at Lowell. There are three canals (along which are situated the factories), so arranged that the water is used three times over—the mills on the upper canal discharging the water from their wheels into the canal of the second level, from the second into the third, and from the third into the river, below the rapids. The upper canal is 140 feet wide, 20 feet deep, and lined on both sides with heavy stone walls. The upper canal is now 5,000 feet in length, the middle 8,000 feet, and the lower 4,000 feet.

They are to be extended when there is demand for more power, and their united length, when completed, will be nearly six miles. The dam, canals, and about 1,000 acres of land are owned by the Holyoke Water-Power Company, who lease the power for a term of years, or in perpetuity, to parties wishing to erect manufacturing establishments. There is never a deficiency of water, even in the driest seasons, nor can the mills on the two upper canals be obstructed by back water, as in some localities.

The project of a dam across the Connecticut, at this place, was first suggested in 1847, and in the following year it was completed, but was so poorly built, that it was carried away a few hours after the gates were closed—just before the water had reached the top of the dam. In 1849 another and much stronger one was built. During the construction of the dam, the water passed through 46 gates, 16 by 18 feet each, and when completed, at twenty-two minutes before one, in the afternoon of October 22, 1849, the engineer gave the signal, and half of them (alternate ones) were closed. Another signal was given, and the remaining gates were shut. The river ceased its flow until its waters, gradually collecting, rose upon the face of the dam, and finally fell in an unbroken sheet over its crest.

This immense volume of water formerly fell perpendicularly over the dam, but the rock in the river below became so much worn, and the timber of which the dam was built, so much injured, that it was necessary to build an apron in front and across the river, fifty feet wide, down which the water now falls, at an angle of about forty-five degrees. The rock in the bed of the river had been worn away to an average depth of thirty feet, by the water falling upon it. The apron was built of timbers, crossing each other at right angles, and the intervening spaces filled with stone. This secures the dam against all possible danger of being carried away. Work upon it was commenced in 1868, and completed in 1871.

Holyoke made slow growth at first; but it has now reached a point from which its future progress is not likely to be checked; and within the last few years its population has largely increased. It now has upwards of 16,000 inhabitants, and in 1873 was incorporated as a city.

More paper is made in Holyoke than in any other place in this country. There are fifteen paper mills, which produce over forty tons daily. Of these, eight manufacture fine writing paper, and seven book, collar, news, tissue, and wrapping paper. There are ninety tons of writing paper made daily in this country, and of this amount, thirty-five tons are made in Holyoke. The other manufactures are envelopes, sheetings, ginghams, woolen goods, thread, alpaca, horseblankets, screws, piano wire, and machinery. The Holyoke Lumber Company, whose mill is above the dam, obtains its logs from the headwaters of the Connecticut. Eight to ten million feet of spruce logs are floated down annually, from which lumber of all dimensions is manufactured.

A free bridge across the Connecticut River connects Holyoke with the village of South Hadley Falls. Holyoke is supplied with water, brought from Ashley Ponds, several miles south-west of the city. A branch railroad connects Holyoke with Westfield, built and operated by the New Haven and Northampton Railroad.

SOUTH HADLEY FALLS.

Opposite Holyoke, is the village of South Hadley Falls. The large brick factory, on the bank of the river, is the Glasgow Gingham works. Leaving Holyoke the tourist passes the dam and around the great bend in the Connecticut, continuing along the bank of the river. The scenery for several miles is particularly fine.

SMITH'S FERRY.—MT. HOLYOKE FEMALE SEMINARY IN THE DISTANCE.

This station is five miles from Holyoke, and four from Northampton. Here passengers for South Hadley cross the Connecticut. The village is in full view, situated on a commanding elevation, about a mile from the river. In South Hadley is located the celebrated Mt. Holyoke Female Seminary, established through the untiring efforts of Mary Lyon, in 1837, who was its first preceptress. The main building is 50 by 94 feet, five stories high, including basement, and has two wings, one at each end. This is strictly a family school on a large scale, to which no day pupils are admitted, and no domestics employed. The labor is divided among the whole number, each young lady having a particular portion of work assigned her, for a given time. The principal object of the institution, is to furnish a supply of well qualified female teachers. Soon after leaving Smith's Ferry, going north, a good view of the Seminary is had, which is situated a short distance south of the village church.

From Smith's Ferry to Northampton, a distance of four miles, the varied objects which can be seen, are of more than usual interest. Nowhere along the whole route, crowded into so small a space, is there so much to attract the attention of the tourist. North and on the right, rises Mount Holyoke, on the summit of which is seen the Prospect House, and on the left is Mt. Tom. Here the Connecticut or the body of water, that once made this region a great lake, gradually wore through the barrier of rock, leaving a magnificent valley, one of the most fertile upon the face of the globe. On the east side of the river, at the western end of Mount Holyoke, are columnar rocks, rising perpendicularly from the water, to the hight of near a hundred feet, which resemble those on the coast of Ireland, forming Fingal's Cave, and the Giant's Causeway. President Hitchcock, in his Geology of Massachusetts, has given them the name of Titan's Pier.

MT. TOM STATION.

Passengers for Mt. Holyoke, Mt. Tom, or Easthampton, leave the cars at this point. A steamer runs from here, to the carriage road, leading to the Holyoke Railway, a mile and a half distant. The carriage road to the summit of Mt. Tom, is only a short distance from the station. Passengers for Easthampton, here take the cars on the branch road, three and a half miles, which make close connections with all the principal trains, from both north and south.

Looking up the Connecticut, on the right, will be noticed Amherst College, eight miles distant. A little to the left, and farther north, is Mount Toby, apparently extending towards the east. A little to the left, and still farther north, is Sugar Loaf Mountain, on the west bank of the Connecticut, and twelve miles from Northampton. After passing over the railroad bridge, to what is known as Ox-Bow Island, the former course of the Connecticut will be seen. Here the river, which formerly made a circuit of three and a half miles, to gain a distance of thirty rods, received the name of Ox-Bow. It curved to the west and thence to the east, coming back to what is now the main channel, east of the bridge. In 1840 a freshet washed through the "neck" east of the railroad, making an island of the land lying in the Bow. While crossing the island, which contains 400 acres, and now connected with the main land by the railroad embankment, can be seen, in the west, the factories and church spires of Easthampton. A saw mill, which turns out from eight to ten million feet of lumber yearly, has been established on Ox-Bow Island. The logs, mostly spruce, are cut on the headwaters of the Connecticut, and are floated down the river in high water. Mr. Stephen Barker, who is the manager of the saw mills at

McIndoe's Falls, on the upper Connecticut, is the leading owner and manager of this mill. South of the Ox-Bow, and under Mt. Tom, is Pascommuck, where, in 1704, nineteen or twenty persons were slain by Indians, and the village burnt. The highest elevation seen west of Easthampton is Pomeroy's Mountain, and at its eastern base are several lead mines that were opened during the Revolution, but owing to the great depth of the ore in the rock, they were abandoned. The meadows north of the Island are very broad, and including those extending to the right, they contain 8000 acres, valued at $150 to $250 per acre. On approaching Northampton, a good view of the State Lunatic Hospital is had, which is located a mile west of the town. In the center will be noticed the High School building, the Town Hall, the First church, and also Round Hill beyond, with its hotel buildings.

MOUNT HOLYOKE.

The first view of Mt. Holyoke, which is situated on the east side of the Connecticut, within two miles of Northampton, when going north, is had, soon after leaving Holyoke. On the summit will be noticed the Prospect House, one thousand feet above the Connecticut. Coming from the north, the mountain is seen at South Deerfield, and most of the way to Northampton, the Prospect House is prominently outlined on the sky beyond. Here in 1821 was built the first house erected on any mountain in New England. It is a favorite place of resort, and during a single season, more than twenty thousand people visit its summit, coming from nearly every northern and western State in the Union. The view is beautiful and picturesque, and is pronounced by distinguished travelers, to be the finest in America. N. P. Willis, and President Hitchcock, the latter distinguished as a geologist, have written glowing descriptions of its unrivaled beauty, while Jenny Lind, during a visit to it when on her

PROSPECT HOUSE, MT. HOLYOKE.

concert tour through this country, spoke of it in terms of unqualified praise. So great a diversity of scenery is rarely met with. Mountain, and meadow, river and valley are harmoniously blended, while here and there the tall spires, of hundreds of churches are seen pointing heavenward. The view is much more extensive than one would suppose, reaching from the Green Mountains, in Vermont, and

Monadnock, in New Hampshire, on the north, to East and West Rocks on the Sound in the south, a distance of more than a hundred miles. On the west, Greylock rears its stately peak, while in the east, the rounded form of Wachusetts meets the eye. The view embraces no less than ten mountains in four States, and about forty villages. But on the whole, the most pleasing scene is that of the river and meadow beneath. The latter diversified by the different crops under cultivation, resembles a magnificent carpet, the beauty and richness of coloring transcending anything produced by art. In looking at this scene, one is reminded more of a great painting than an actual landscape. The proprietor of the Prospect House, J. W. French, has resided on the mountain nearly thirty years. The present house is 55 by 70 feet, two stories high. Visitors are taken to the summit by steam power, an inclined railway having been constructed in 1854, extending 600 feet down the mountain to the carriage road. A steamboat makes trips on the Connecticut, carrying passengers between the base of the mountain and Mt. Tom station on the Connecticut River Railroad. The summit is less than three miles from Northampton, from which place it is easily reached by carriage, or by railroad and steamboat.

Mt. Holyoke was named in 1654, after Capt. Elizur Holyoke, one of the first proprietors of Northampton, and it is stated that Mt. Tom, on the opposite (west) side of the Connecticut River, received its named from one Rowland Thomas. There are various traditions concerning this matter, but the following, as stated by Dr. Holland in his history of Western Massachusetts, is the most probable, as well as quite poetical: "A company of the first settlers of Springfield went northward to explore the country. The party headed by Elizur Holyoke went up on the east side of the river, and another headed by Rowland Thomas went up on the west side. The parties arriving abrest, at the narrow place in the river below Hockanum, at what is now called Rock Ferry, Holyoke and Thomas held a conversation with one another across the river, and each, then and there, gave his name to the mountain at whose feet he stood. The name of Holyoke remains uncorrupted and without abbreviation, while Mount Thomas has been curtailed to simple and homely 'Tom.'"

The serpentine course of the Connecticut River, forms a very attractive feature of the view from the mountain; but one of the greatest objects of interest is the old Ox-Bow, which receives its name from the peculiar course of the river, a mile below Hockanum Ferry and near the base of Mt. Tom. It formerly ran more westerly around a narrow strip of land, coming back directly opposite the place where the angle was made, and thence southerly, between Mounts Holyoke and Tom. The distance across the neck, from bank to bank, was only thirty rods, while the river in making the circuit, ran three and a half miles. The boatmen on the river, had frequently endeavored to get permission to cut a channel through and change the course of the river; but the owners objected, as it would greatly discommode them. High water, however, accomplished what the boatmen failed to secure. On the 24th of February, 1840, the ice broke up and gorged in the river at the end of the "Bow," which caused the

THE OX-BOW—FROM MT. HOLYOKE.

water to set back. It continued to rise till it ran over the "neck." A few furrows had been plowed on the "neck" during the previous autumn, and as the frost was out of the ground, a channel was soon cut through to the river below. A large number of acres were washed away, and the whole course of the river was changed. This made an island of the Ox-Bow, and it so remained till it was connected to the main land by the railroad embankment. There are 400 acres in Ox-Bow Island, as it is now called, although viewing it from the mountain with the naked eye, it does not have the appearance of containing upward of 100. Before the new channel was formed the Ox-Bow Meadows were within the limits of the town of Hadley, but by an act of the Legislature it became part of Northampton.

THE CONNECTICUT—FROM MT. HOLYOKE.

The view of the meadows from the mountain is particularly fine. Directly below and along the base of the mountain runs the Connecticut. Beyond are the meadows, and on the western aclivity and reaching to them, is situated Northampton. Its church spires, thickly clustered cottages, and business blocks make a pleasing landscape. North is the winding river, broad meadows and the villages of Hadley,

Hatfield, Whately, with Sugar Loaf Mountain rising in the center of the valley.

MOUNT TOM.

Mount Tom, on the west side of the Connecticut, will be noticed in the north-west, soon after leaving Springfield. The point seen, which is the southern end, is 1,200 feet high, the greatest elevation of any part of the mountain range. The south-

THE CONNECTICUT—FROM MT. TOM.

eastern face is comparatively gradual in ascent, and reaches nearly down to the Connecticut. The northwestern side is more precipitous, and in some places is nearly perpendicular. It is some three or four miles in length, and its northern end terminates within a few rods of the Connecticut, opposite Mt. Holyoke, which is now known as Mt. Nonotuck. William Street built a house on the eastern part of Mt. Tom, in 1866, a half mile from Mt. Tom Station, for the accommodation of visitors. The view of the meadows and the river is exceedingly beautiful from this point. A carriage road extends nearly to the summit.

NEWHAVEN—WILLIAMSBURG.

New York, 74; Plainville, 27; Westfield, 61; Holyoke, 71; Easthampton, 72; Northampton, 76; Williamsburg, 84 miles.

The New Haven and Northampton Railroad follows closely the line of the old Farmington Canal, which was abandoned about thirty years ago. It passes through a thriving region, and the towns along its route are some of the best in Connecticut and Massachusetts. The principal stations, on the main line, taken in their order, after leaving New Haven, are Cheshire, Southington, Plainville, Farmington, Avon, Simsbury, Granby, Westfield, Southampton, Easthampton, Northampton, Florence, Leeds, and Williamsburg; and on the branches are Collinsville and New Hartford, in Connecticut, and Holyoke, in Massachusetts. At Cheshire, fifteen miles from New Haven, there is a flourishing Episcopal school and considerable capital invested in manufacturing interests. Southington, twenty-two miles from New Haven, is largely engaged in manufacturing, and is one of the most important stations on the road. At Plainville, the Hartford, Providence and Fishkill Railroad crosses the New Haven and Northampton Railroad. Farmington village lies east of the railroad, nine miles north of Southington. At this place there is an old and well-known School for young ladies, kept by Miss

Porter, a sister of Dr. Porter, President of Yale College, whose patrons come from the wealthiest families in the country. A branch road extends from Farmington to New Hartford, following Farmington river, and passing through Collinsville, where are manufactured, by the Collins Company, axes, plows, and various other agricultural implements for the Spanish and South American trade. This is one of the largest manufacturing companies in New England, and its sales amount to nearly a million of dollars annually. The company has been engaged in the manufacture of axes nearly fifty years, and employs about five hundred hands. The town derives its support mainly from the employes of the Company. Here is one of the best country hotels in New England, and, during the summer, is filled with city boarders. Going north from Farmington, and east of Avon, will be noticed Wadsworth Tower, on Talcott Mountain. From it there is a splendid view, extending to the Sound on the south. It can be easily reached from Avon station, and will well repay a visit. Five miles north of Avon is Simsbury. Here is the crossing of the Connecticut Western Railroad, which extends from Hartford to Millerton, N. Y. There is some manufacturing done at Granby, five miles north of Simsbury, but the people are mostly engaged in Agricultural pursuits. Westfield, sixty-one miles from New Haven, is noted for the manufacture of cigars, whips, organs, and paper. The Boston and Albany Railroad is crossed at this place, and a branch road extends from here to Holyoke, a distance of ten miles. Southampton, nine miles north of Westfield, is the birthplace of ex-Senator Pomeroy, of Kansas, and it is, also, distinguished for having educated more young men for the ministry, and made more cider brandy, than any other town in the Commonwealth. About forty persons, natives of this town, were college-educated, and entered the ministry. The manufacture of cider brandy, once a large industry, was abandoned many years ago. There is considerable capital invested in the manufacture of whips in this town. There is, also, a silver and lead mine, which has been worked, at various times, for nearly a hundred years. Some very fine specimens of both silver and lead have been found, but not yet in paying quantities.

EASTHAMPTON.

Easthampton is in every sense a representative New England town. Its industrial interests and educational institutions have made it well known, and truly represent New England thrift and culture. Its growth and good name are mainly due to Hon. Samuel Williston, who laid the foundation of its well-known school, and its manufactories. Mr. Williston is a son of Rev. Payson Williston, the first minister of the town, who was settled in 1789. At an early day, Mr. Williston commenced the manufacture of buttons, and, from a small beginning, has grown an extensive business. The first factory was built in 1848, and, at the present time, there are over a million and a-half dollars invested in the

OFFICE AND FACTORY OF THE NASHAWANNUCK COMPANY.

various manufacturing interests that have sprung from this modest beginning. Mr. Williston has been ably assisted by younger gentlemen, who have carried forward the work that he laid out, and their combined efforts have produced good results. Mr. Williston was making sewed buttons as early as 1827, giving them out to a thousand families, residing in adjacent towns. Subsequently, machinery was invented, and the business wholly done in the factory in Easthampton. Hon. H. G. Knight and Seth Warner were admitted to partnership, and the business was conducted under the firm name of Williston, Knight & Co., and subsequently was incorporated the present National Button Company, which is now the largest manufactory of its kind in the country. Over 300 kinds, and 1800 gross are manufactured daily. One hundred thousand dollars' worth of material is used annually, and the product reaches a quarter of a million dollars in value. Mr. Williston is president, and Mr. Knight treasurer of the Company. The capital stock of the Company is $150,000.

The manufacture of suspenders was commenced in 1849, and for many years there was hardly a farmer's family within twenty miles of Easthampton, wherein the good wife did not, in her leisure hours, make suspenders for Mr. Williston, he furnishing the webbing. In 1852 this interest was converted into a Stock Company, under the name of Nashawannuck Manufacturing Company, and has now a capital of $300,000. Three hundred hands are employed, and four thousand pairs of suspenders are made weekly. Mr. Williston is president, and E. H. Sawyer treasurer and agent of the Company. The goods are sold in New York by Sawyer and Judson, C. Judson, who is a stockholder and director of the Company, superintends this part of the business. Store at 76 Worth st.

In 1859, Mr. Williston built a factory for the purpose of manufacturing cotton yarn to supply the Nashawannuck Company, and this has become the largest manufacturing interest in the town. Three hundred and fifty hands are employed, and a million pounds of cotton are annually transformed into yarn. The Capital is $350,000. The Company consists of Mr. Williston, E. H. Sawyer, and M. H. Leonard.

The Glendale Elastic Fabric Company, which now makes elastic braided and woven goods, and the only successful manufacturers of woven goring for Congress Boots, in this country, had its origin in the visit of Mr. Sawyer to Europe, in 1859. Moses H. Leonard is treasurer of this Company, and W. Z. Wooster, agent.

The Easthampton Rubber-Thread Company was organized in 1864, mainly to supply the demands of the Easthampton factories. The Capital is $150,000, and the daily product one thousand pounds of thread. H. G. Knight is president, and E. Thomas Sawyer treasurer and agent.

The Mt. Tom Thread Company, and the Valley Machine Company, are younger institutions, but are doing a successful business. It will be noticed that it has been the aim of Mr. Williston and his associates, to produce from the raw material, everything that enters into the various goods produced by them, and in this way they have been able to successfully extend their manufacturing interests, simply by supplying the demand created by the first factory that was established.

WILLISTON SEMINARY.

Material interests have not here overshadowed higher aims. Mr. Williston has devoted his time largely to establishing manufacturing interests; but his great success has given him means to carry forward other noble works. Williston Seminary, is one of these. He was early interested in the cause of education, and in 1841, procured the passage of an act, incorporating Williston Seminary. From time to time he has given liberally of his means, to increase the standing and worth of this institution. Up to the present time he has given $270,000 to the Seminary, and it is understood that he has made provisions in his will, for giving nearly as much more, so as to place it on a foundation that will make it far superior to any classical school in this country, for fitting young men for college, or preparing them for a practical business life. The original Seminary building was burned in 1857, after which the present South Hall was erected. Middle Hall was built in 1844. The beautiful Hall for the Gymnasium in 1864; and North Hall in 1866. The principal of the Seminary is Dr. Marshall Henshaw, who is assisted by an able corps of teachers, and no efforts are spared to make this the leading school in the country. Among its graduates are gentlemen who have won success in science and literature, and in the practical affairs of the country.

Easthampton has also good churches, and an elegant Town Hall, the latter a credit to any town in New England, and well suited to the needs of the place. The view from the tower, which is 133 feet high, is very fine.

HILL'S MANSION HOUSE.

No town is complete without a first-class hotel, and in this respect, Easthampton is particularly favored. Mr. William Hill, the proprietor of Hill's Mansion House, has no superior as a landlord, and few equals. For many years he kept the Mansion House at Northampton. In 1869 he went to Easthampton, purchased his present Hotel, and has since increased its capacity from fifty to a hundred and fifty rooms, and its yearly receipts from $8000 to $40,000. The Hotel is well situated for the accommodation of summer travel. Passengers can come or go by the express trains, on the New Haven and Northampton Railroad, twice daily to and from New York, without change of cars, taking and leaving the cars in the Grand Central Depot in New York. There is also connection with all the trains on the Connecticut River Railroad, at Mt. Tom station by the branch road from Easthampton to Mt. Tom. White Mountain travelers can leave New York at 3 o'clock in the afternoon, stop over night at Easthampton, and proceed the next morning. Coming from the north, they can leave the White Mountains in the morning, stop over night at Mr. Hill's, and reach New York about noon, or later, the next day.

HILL'S MANSION HOUSE, EASTHAMPTON.

The Connecticut, the broad meadows, Mt. Holyoke and the distant eastern range of hills are seen soon after leaving Easthampton. The State Lunatic Hospital, north of the railroad, is passed before entering Northampton, from the grounds of which, there is a fine view. From Northampton to Williamsburg, a distance of eight miles, there is almost a continuous line of villages. Florence, Leeds, Haydenville, Skinnerville and Williamsburg, before the calamity of May 16, 1874, were remarkably prosperous and enterprising manufacturing villages.

THE MILL RIVER DISASTER.

Saturday morning, May 16, 1874, is a memorable morning to those who lived in the Mill River Valley, and the great loss of life, and the destruction of property, which followed the breaking away of the Williamsburg reservoir, is without a parallel, in the history of New England. Large manufacturing establishments, stores and private dwellings, were swept away in almost an instant, almost before warning could be given, and many persons were hurried into eternity. The number of lives lost so far as known is 141. The bodies of 137 were recovered, and 4 others, known to have been lost, were never found.

Mill River rises in Goshen and Conway, and empties into the Connecticut just below Northampton, some fifteen miles from its source. Between Williamsburg and Northampton, a distance of eight miles, large and thriving manufacturing establishments had been built, which depended upon the waters of Mill River for power. In the summer months, the river often became low, and the various mill owners caused a reservoir to be built, upon the east branch three miles north of Williamsburg, in which was held a surplus of water, to be let out as required. Another had previously been built in Goshen, on the

Names of the Lost in the Flood of May 16th, 1874.

WILLIAMSBURG.

Mrs Susan M. Lamb, 54,—Wife of George E. Lamb.
George Ashley, 16.
E. C. Hubbard, 56.
Emma C. Wood, 25,—of Chicopee, and her son Harold H. Wood, 1.
Dr. Elbridge M. Johnson, 36; Mrs. Mary F. Johnson; Edward M. Johnson, 8; Mary H. Johnson, 6; Charlotte Johnson, 4; Mrs. Johnson, 60, Mother of Dr. Johnson. —The entire family lost.
Theodore J. Hitchcock, 34.
William H. Adams, 51.
Archie Lancour, 21.
Mrs. E. M. Chandler, 39; Mary Chandler, 9 —

HAYDENVILLE AND SKINNERVILLE.

Mrs. Sarah Hillman, 38.
Mrs. Christiana Hills, 46.
Eli Bryant, 73
Robert Hayden, 5.
Mrs. Mary Morris, 56.
Johanna Williams, 22.
Francis Brodeur, 20.
Grace Thayer, 5; Freddie Thayer, 8 months.
John L. Kaplinger, 76.
Mrs. Mary Hogan, 50.
Edward Monkler, 60.
Agnes Miller, 10; George Miller, 8; Willie Miller, 1.
Mrs. Margaret Wilson, 44; Matilda Wilson, 11; Rosa Wilson, 7; Margaret Wilson, 4.

west branch, and had materially benefited the manufacturers. An act of incorporation was procured, and work upon the reservoir was commenced in 1865. In the following season it was completed. The dam was built principally of earth, a narrow stone wall in the center was carried up from the bottom nearly to the top, for the purpose of preventing animals from working through the embankment. The dam was four hundred feet long and fifty-five feet high in the center, and when full, 125 acres were flooded to the average depth of twenty-five feet. It had leaked considerably at times, but the owners had generally regarded it as safe. A gate keeper lived at the reservoir to raise and lower the gate as the wants of the mills below for increased or diminished supply of water demanded, and to report all indications of danger. For nearly three years previous to the disaster, George Cheney acted as gate keeper. Just before seven o'clock on the morning of the 16th, Mr. Cheney's father happened to look out of the window and saw the earth commence to slide from the lower face of the dam, east of the center. His son went immediately to the dam, but before he reached it a strip of earth forty feet long, had slid into the ravine below. As fast as possible he went down the embankment below the dam, and raised the gate at the peril of his own life. He then hurried to the barn just south of his house, and mounted his horse to give warning to the inhabitants in Williamsburg. As fast as the animal could carry him, he went down the narrow valley along the river road to Williamsburg, reporting immediately to Mr. O. G. Spelman, the condition of the dam. He reached Williamsburg in about fifteen minutes, but Mr. Spelman, whose duty it was to look after the dam, had so much confidence in its strength, that he did not apparently credit the report, and some few moments were lost in discussing the subject with Mr. Cheney, who insisted upon having the people warned against the approaching danger. He was finally directed by Mr. Spelman to go to Mr. Belcher's for another horse. Meantime Collins Graves, the village milkman, drove up, and learning that the dam had broken away started for Haydenville, to give the alarm. Cheney was going on a like errand, but before he could secure a fresh horse, the water came down the valley into Williamsburg. Further progress was prevented and he was obliged to turn back to save his life. In almost an instant after the water made its first appearance, it struck Mr. Spelman's button factory, and the mill owned by W. H. Adams and J. T. Hitchcock, and dashed them to attoms. On it went, carrying everything before it, and leaving desolation in its path. Trees of many year's growth, and strong buildings were only as reeds, and instantly went down before the advancing wave. The crashing sound of the wrecked buildings, and the wails of the drowning inmates, went up seemingly from every hand, while the inhabitants not in peril, were paralized with fear, and stood almost mute and motionless. The stream was so great and so rapid, that when it reached the valley, below Spelman's button factory, where the channel turns to the left, it leaped across the bank, and cut an entirely new one through the beautiful and fertile meadows beyond. The cottages that lined the street were swept away, and nearly all their inmates were lost. On this once beautiful spot, between the main part of the village and the depot, twenty-six dwellings were carried away, and sixty persons lost their lives. The woolen mill owned by Henry L. James was damaged, but escaped destruction.

Collins Graves, who started for Haydenville to give the alarm, stopped at William Skinner's silk factory and notified the operatives of the impending danger, and then proceeded to Haydenville. Myron Day was going from Leeds to Haydenville, and seeing the water coming, returned to give notice of the approaching wave. He drove rapidly down the river road, just in advance of the coming flood, and reached Leeds only a few minutes before the buildings were swept off. He alarmed all whom he saw, and barely had time to escape to the higher ground before the terrible shock came. Jerome Hillman did efficient work in spreading the alarm. He had been to Haydenville, from Skinnerville, after the mail for the silk factory, and was about midway between the two places, when he saw the great wave coming down the valley. He turned around and drove as rapidly as possible to the Haydenville church and rang the bell, thereby giving the first general alarm, which was the means of saving many lives. After the wave had passed, he returned to his own home to find that his house had been moved from its foundation, and his wife drowned, while attempting to escape to the high ground.

After the water had passed through Williamsburg, it kept on its course down the valley, sweeping every thing before it, uprooting immense trees and crushing everything in its path. Dwelling houses and immense factories were crushed like egg shells, and went down the stream to add weight to the great column that was moving with such rapidity and power. It struck Mr. Skinner's silk factory first. The operatives had received warning, and barely reached the high ground in safety. The building resisted, for a moment, the force, then crumbled away and disappeared forever from sight. Twenty or more dwellings—half of which were the property of Mr. Skinner—yielded to the immense wave, and were soon broken in pieces. His beautiful and costly home stemmed the fearful torrent, though it was badly injured; and this was all that was left to Mr. Skinner of a handsome fortune—the accumulated earnings of a lifetime. It was scarcely five minutes from the first warning to the time the mill was swept away.

Several dwellings, below Mr. Skinner's, were the next to be carried off. At Haydenville, the extensive works of Hayden, Gere & Co., in which 300 hands were employed in manufacturing brass fittings, and their substantial office building, occupied in part by the Haydenville Savings Bank, afforded

Nonotuck Silk Factory, at Leeds.

Mr. Skinner's Residence.

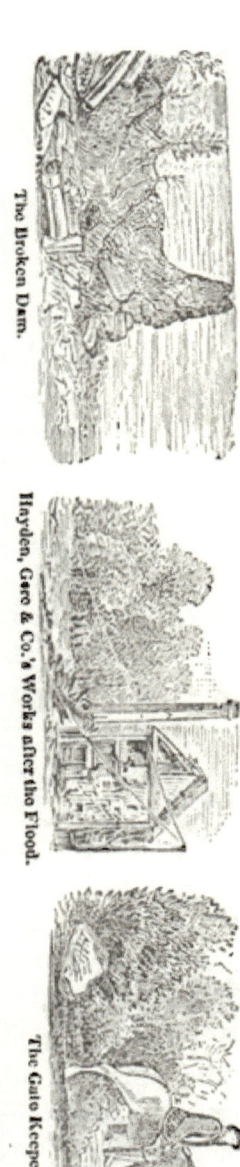
The Broken Dam.

Warner's Button Factory at Leeds.

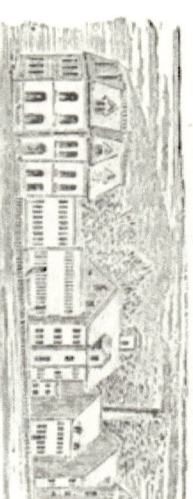
Hayden, Gere & Co.'s Works before the Flood.

Hayden, Gere & Co.'s Works after the Flood.

Cook's Dam, at Leeds.

A Wrecked House at Haydenville.

The Gate Keeper.

no resistance, and it was only a few minutes before they crumbled away and were lost. Stores and dwellings were next carried away. The Diamond Tobacco Factory shared the same fate, and onward swept the mighty current, increasing in power as it was compressed into smaller space in the narrow valley. Reaching Leeds everything gave way before it. The dam and boarding house of the Nonotuck Silk Factory, private dwellings and the large Button Factory of George P. Warner, were instantly destroyed. The warning of its approach had hardly reached the village before it was doing its work of destruction. No time was given for preparation and the occupants of the dwellings were cut off from escape. Below Leeds, the valley is wider and this, in a measure, retarded the progress of the flood, but its force was not entirely spent till it reached the Connecticut, more than ten miles from the reservoir. The loss of life was so great and so unexpected, that those who escaped seemed paralized after the work of destruction was over, and for weeks none could realize the terrible reality. The first sight of the flood was frightful in the extreme. A wall of debris, thirty feet high, was seen moving down the valley with great rapidity, while a cloud of dust and spray rose high in the air, conveying the impression that a great fire was raging in the distance. A better understanding of the velocity of the flood can be had by remembering that the bottom of the reservoir was 313 feet above the streets of Williamsburg, a rise of over 100 feet in a mile.

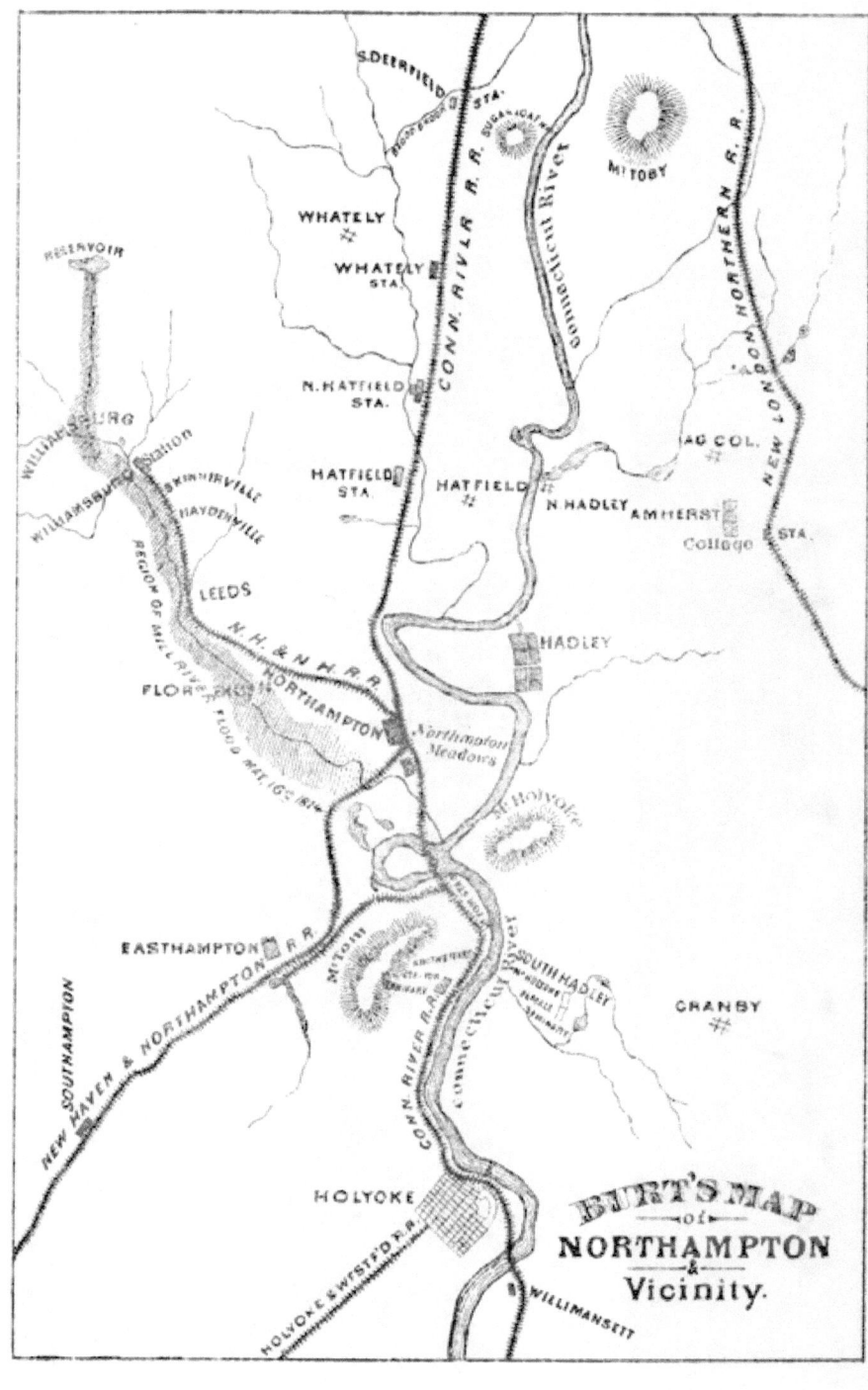

NORTHAMPTON.

New York, 153; White Mountains, 167; Lake Memphremagog, 212; Montreal, 293; Quebec, 373 miles.

NORTHAMPTON, which is 17 miles from Springfield, is among the oldest towns in the Connecticut Valley, having been settled in 1654, by 21 planters from Hartford and Windsor, who purchased it of the Indians for "one hundred fathoms of wampum, ten coats and some small gifts." The Indian name of the town is Nonotuck. The whites gave it the name of Northampton, after a town of the same name in England. There are few villages in New England which present so many attractions to the summer tourist, and few are so widely and favorably known. A traveler writing of it, very appropriately remarks: "We must peep at Northampton with loving leisure. It is the frontispiece of the book of beauty, which nature opens wide in the valley of the Connecticut, and one of the most winsome pictures in the volume." Its broad and extensive meadows, its river and mountain scenery, its ancient elms and shaded streets, distinguish it from all the other towns on the banks of the noble Connecticut. It has always been noted for its culture and refinement, as well as for its great natural beauty, and many distinguished men have been among its residents, including Maj. Joseph Hawley, a distinguished lawyer and statesman, who died in 1788; Rev. Jonathan Edwards, the third minister of the town, who preached here 23 years, from 1727 to 1753; and Gov. Caleb Strong, who was a member of the provincial Congress in 1774, of the Convention for drafting the Constitution of the United States, and one of the committee to draft a Constitution to be submitted to the people; a member of the United States Senate in the first Congress, and for eleven years Governor of Massachusetts, commencing in 1800. In the cemetery are buried four persons who served as United States Senators from Massachusetts, and also were residents of Northampton, Gov. Cabel Strong, Eli P. Ashmun, Elijah H. Mills and Isaac C. Bates. The latter who died at Washington in 1844, while occupying his seat in the Senate, was one of the most eloquent and able men who have represented Massachusetts at Washington. Dr. Sylvester Graham, one of the first lecturers on health in this country, was also buried in this cemetery. He resided many years in Northampton, and was a man of great intellectual and philosophic power, and although misunderstood and misrepresented, his teachings have turned the public attention towards the importance of observing the laws of health. The Edwards' Elm on King Street, the top of which can be seen west of the railroad, shortly after crossing Main Street, is among the oldest and most beautiful trees in Northampton. It was set out by President Edwards, in front of his dwelling, during his ministry in the town.

Northampton is unusually favored with educational and benevolent institutions, which will give the place great prominence. In addition to the bequests of Oliver Smith, of Hatfield, who died in 1845, leaving a large property to be devoted to public charities, and to the founding of an agricultural school in Northampton, 60 years after his death, John Clarke who was a native and resident of the town, died in 1870, leaving a large estate to endow a school for the deaf and dumb, known as Clarke Institute. He had previously given the school $50,000, which had received his name, and at his death he left upwards of $400,000 more to carry forward the work that had been begun. A site was purchased on Round Hill, and suitable buildings erected for the school, which is now in successful operation. The pupils are taught to articulate, and great progress has been made in teaching this unfortunate class. Miss Sophia Smith of Hatfield, an aged maiden lady, and niece of Oliver Smith, the founder of the Smith Charities, died in 1870, leaving nearly a half million of dollars, to endow the Smith College, at Northampton, for females. Grounds have been purchased just west of the business center, and suitable buildings are to be erected so as to open the school in September, 1875. It is intended to make this one of the best educational institutions in the country, not to be surpassed by the best Colleges for young men. The President of the College is L. Clarke Seelye, formerly professor in Amherst College. Northampton, with its own educational institutions, is certainly highly favored, for its nearness to other institutions of learning. On the west is Easthampton with its Williston Seminary, one of the best schools for fitting young men for College. On the south is South Hadley with its famous Mt. Holyoke Female Seminary, founded by that devout woman, Mary Lyon, On the east, and in full view, is Amherst College, well known through out the country, and the Massachusetts State Agricultural College, the most successful institution of its kind in the country. With these facilities near at hand, for procuring the very best education, the young men and women of the town ought not to grow up in ignorance. Through the instrumentalities of various individuals, Northampton is now in the possession of a valuable public library, free to every resident of the town, and ample provisions have been made for its maintenance. John Clarke, the founder of the Clarke Institute for the deaf and dumb, left $40,000, the income of which is to be used to purchase new books. A library building, known as Memorial Hall, has been built at an expense of $75,000, and it is one of the finest buildings in New England, for library purposes, and is an honor to the town.

ROUND HILL AND ITS HOTEL.

Round Hill, a beautiful eminence overlooking the town, with its Hotel buildings, and its grove of native forest trees, will be noticed in the north-west before reaching the town, and about a quarter of a mile west of the railroad. Here George Bancroft, the historian, and J. G. Coggswell, for some years

ROUND HILL, NORTHAMPTON, MASS.

Librarian of the Astor Library, had a famous classical school—one of the most noted in this country. Jenny Lind spent several months here just after her marriage, previous to returning to Europe. The Round Hill Hotel, formerly a Water Cure, has under its present management taken first rank among the Family Summer Resorts of the country. The location has been long and favorably known as one of rare attractions, presenting a combination of beautiful meadow, town, and mountain scenery, extensive groves and lawns, pure air, and water, which are rarely if ever found at one place elsewhere, and which caused Jenny Lind to christen this place the "Paradise of America," and the poet to sing:

> "Queen village of the meads
> Fronting the sun-rise and in beauty throned,
> With jeweled homes around her lifted brow,
> And coronal of ancient forest trees,—
> Northampton sits and rules her pleasant realm."

From the Hotel are the drives to Mt. Holyoke, Hockanum, Mt. Nonotuck, Mt. Tom, Sugar Loaf Mt. Toby, Amherst, Easthampton, Holyoke City, South Hadley, and Florence, all places of interest in themselves. This Hotel is nearest Leeds, Haydenville, Skinnerville and Williamsburg, the scene of the Mill River disaster. Terms are very reasonable. The New York Evening Post says: "This Hotel is very delightful and as the merits of the place have become known, its patronage has rapidly increased."

THE C. F. SIMONDS HOTEL COMPANY.

The Fitch Hotel, on Main Street, built on the site of the old Warner House, destroyed by fire a few years since, is managed by The C. F. Simonds Hotel Company, with C. F. Simonds as its landlord who has had long experience, and provides bountifully for his guests. It is the only hotel in the business part of the town. A livery stable is connected with the Hotel.

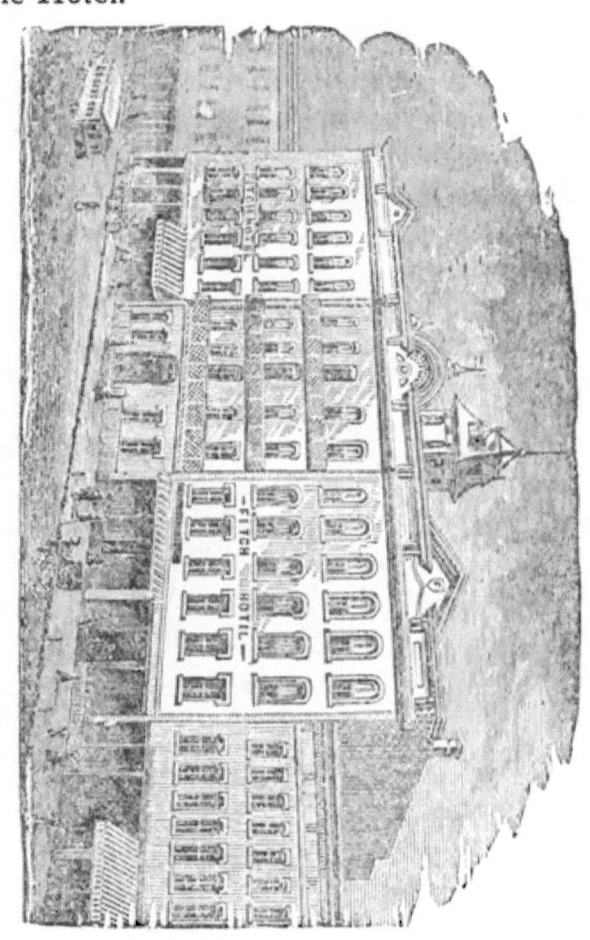

FITCH HOTEL, NORTHAMPTON, MASS.

The State Lunatic Hospital, located one mile west of the village, is a large structure. The erection of the building was commenced in 1856, and completed in 1858. The length of the two wings and main building is 512 feet. The wings are three stories high, and the main building four. The floors cover an area of four acres. The first Superintendent was Dr. William Henry Prince, of Salem. Resigning in 1864, Dr. Pliny Earle, formerly Superintendent of the Bloomingdale Hospital, was appointed Superintendent, which position he now holds. Its average number of patients is about 450.

THE SMITH CHARITIES.

Oliver Smith, of Hatfield, a bachelor, died in 1845 worth $370,000, which he left by will to be devoted principally to charitable objects. Among the provisions of the will was the establishment of the Smith's Agricultural School at Northampton, 60 years after his decease, and to assist poor and worthy young men and women, and widow ladies. The will provides that young men and women, taken from families residing in Northampton, Williamsburg, Hatfield, Hadley and Amherst, in Hampshire County, and in Whately, Deerfield and Greenfield, in Franklin County, and bound out to persons residing in those towns, shall receive: girls, when married, as a marriage portion, the sum of $300; boys, when of age, a loan of $500 for five years—interest to be paid annually. At the end of the five years, if they prove themselves worthy, then they shall have the $500 outright, as a present to assist them in commencing business. Under certain conditions, the will also provides that indigent young women, about to be married, can have $50 as a marriage portion,

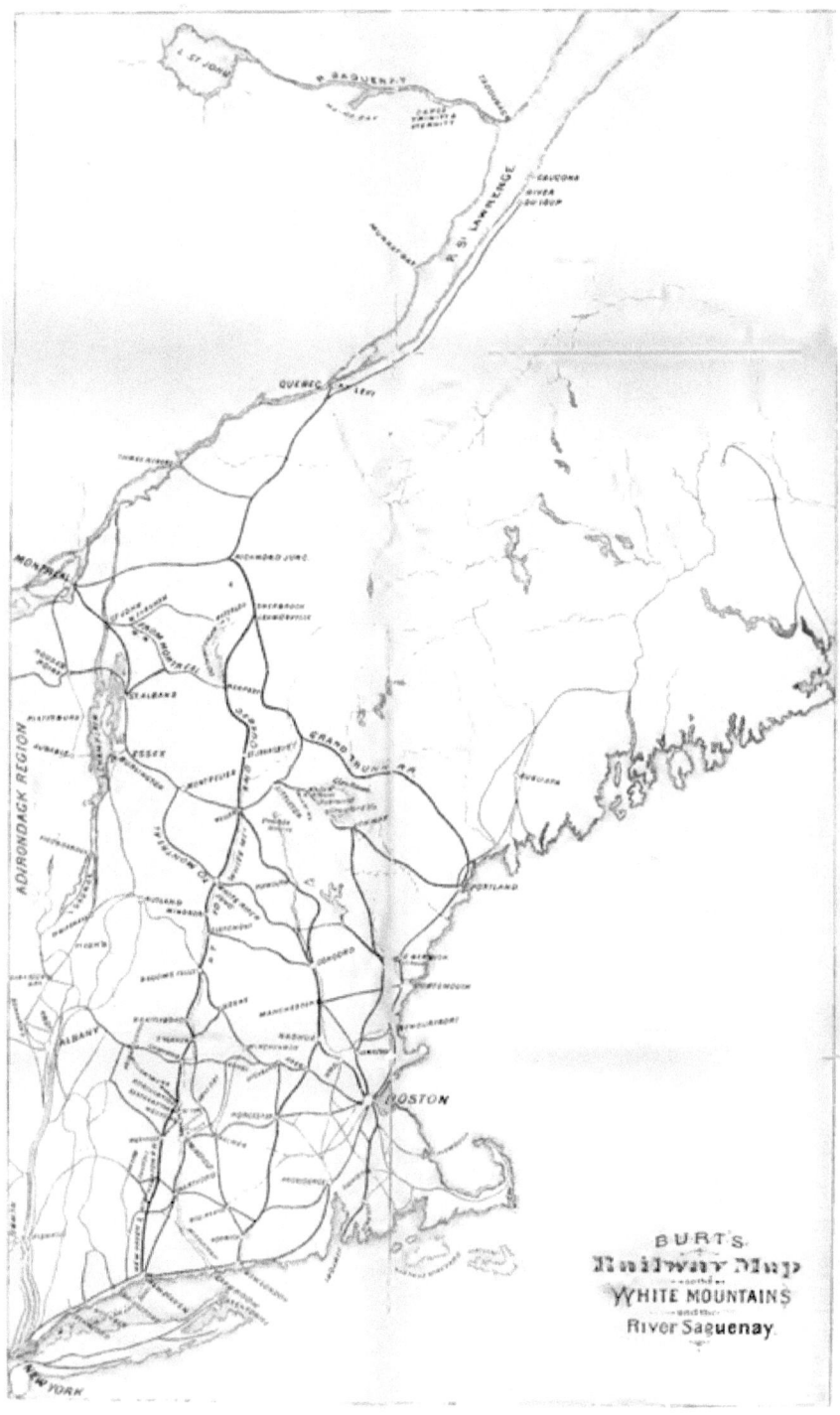

and that indigent widows, who have children dependent upon them, can receive $50 annually, to assist them in supporting their families. The aggregate amount of the several funds is now over one million dollars. A considerable portion of the income is given away annually in accordance with the provisions of the will.

THE SILK FEVER AND ITS ORIGIN.

The speculative mania which swept over this country some 30 or 40 years ago, concerning the production of raw silk, had its origin in Northampton. The motive, however, of the one who suggested it, was not of a speculative nature, but had its foundation in a desire to do a great public good. The originator of it has had remarkable experience, and his history is of more than ordinary interest. Mr. Samuel Whitmarsh, the gentleman referred to, was formerly a dry goods merchant in New York. In 1830 he went to Northampton to reside. It occurring to him that the production of raw silk might be successfully achieved in this country, he traveled through the silk regions of the Old World to make investigations. He returned home with full belief in its practicability, and at once made arrangements to commence the business in Northampton. Mulberry trees were planted and cocooneries established. The subject was then discussed in the public prints, and thousands rushed into the business without any knowledge of it. Speculators seized upon it and fanned the flame, and it became a mania, running through the country like wild-fire. As a natural result, the whole thing proved a failure. A company was formed in Northampton and a factory was established in the village of Florence for the manufacture of silk. In that factory was woven cloth for a silk vest which Mr. Whitmarsh presented to Henry Clay. In Northampton a smaller factory was also built, and in it ribbons of various qualities were woven. After making a series of experiments, Mr. Whitmarsh became satisfied that a warmer climate would be more favorable to the production of raw silk. He went to the island of Jamaica to make investigations, and was convinced that the business could be successfully carried on there. He formed a company with a capital of $200,000, and in 1848 erected extensive buildings. Through the various discouragements that intervened, Mr. Whitmarsh never wavered. He visited England to interest the people in the enterprise, and while at London sold $50,000 worth of stock in the Company. The samples of silk he had with him were pronounced to be the best in the London market. Lord Metcalf, just appointed Governor of Jamaica, took great interest in the enterprise, and declared to Mr. Whitmarsh that he was deserving of the highest monument that could be erected, for what he had already accomplished. Returning to Jamaica, to his great chagrin and disappointment, he found that one of the directors in the Company had had some difficulty with the owners of an ice house, in which the worms had been placed, and had removed them to a cellar, the dampness of which had killed them. As they had long been undergoing the process of acclimation, this put the enterprise back five years. Following this began a long and unprofitable litigation, and finally the project was abandoned altogether. In 1846 he loaded a small vessel with tropical plants, orange trees, century plants, &c., and accompanied with his family and some 30 American workmen, sailed from Jamaica for Boston, with a view of opening a botanical garden, under the patronage of the city, the ship and cargo being all that was left of a large property, and what at one time promised a magnificent fortune. In Boston, the proposition to establish a conservatory and garden did not meet with success, and it was abandoned. Before leaving Jamaica he took up a century plant, and sailed for London, where he sold it for a hundred guineas, and returned home by the same steamer.

Florence, a village within the limits of the town, and about two miles and a half west of the center, in point of business has perhaps shown the greatest enterprise. Here are located the shops of the Florence Sewing Machine Company, the Nonotuck Silk Company, a Brush factory, Cotton factory, &c. Dr. Charles Munde, a participator in the German revolutions, and a refugee, for many years, had a water-cure establishment here, but it was burnt in 1865, and he subsequently returned to Europe to educate his children, having received a pardon from the King, and an appointment under our government. Some years ago there was an industrial association in Florence, called the Community, similar to those advocated by Fourier, the distinguished French philanthropist. Considerable land was purchased and held by the association. Here was gathered some of the brightest intellects of the country, who joined the association to achieve an ideal life. Failing to make it pecuniarily self-sustaining, the project was abandoned, but some of its members still reside in the town, and are among its best and most worthy citizens.

The population of Northampton is over 11,000. Besides the Connecticut River Railroad, the New Haven and Northampton Railroad passes through the town, terminating at Williamsburg, six miles to the north-west. The Massachusetts Central Railroad, extending from Northampton to Boston, is in process of construction. The town is also supplied with excellent water, brought about five miles from the west part of the town.

Four distinguished authors—Henry Ward Beecher, Lydia Maria Child, Oliver Wendell Holmes, and Dr. J. G. Holland—have each laid the scenes of popular novels, written by them, in this beautiful town.

Tom O'Keefe, of Northampton, who is a rollicking, six-foot Irishman, and a well-known frequenter of the jail, was arrested one day for drunkenness, and, on arriving at the foot of the long steps leading to the entrance of that institution, in a state of intoxication, refused to walk farther. Mr. Banks then jailer, came out and tried to induce Tom to ascend the steps, who settled back and said: "Mr.

TOM ENTERTAINS SERIOUS DOUBTS.

Banks, this *may* be a good boarding place, but I have *divilish* strong suspicions to the contrary."

HADLEY.

Both above and below Northampton, the church spires of Old Hadley can be seen, about three miles east of the railroad, the streets of which extend from the Connecticut on the north, to the same river on the south, a distance of about a mile, the town lying in the neck or base of the peninsular. The Connecticut here makes a curve to the west, and thence to the east in its southerly course of seven miles. The town was settled in 1650, by a colony from Hartford, Windsor and Wethersfield, Conn. There are three streets running north and south, parallel with each other. West street was laid out before the colony came to the town, with "home lots" of several acres each, on either side of the street, which was originally twenty rods wide and one mile in length. In 1773 the original width was reduced to eighteen rods. Since that time still furthur reductions have been made, which have cut it down to seventeen and one-half rods at the South, and fifteen and one-half rods at the North. Various causes, including the encroachments of the river at the north end, have reduced its length to 300 rods, consequently it contains not far from twenty-one acres. On each side of the street are two rows of ancient elms, nearly 1,000 in number; and the quiet, rural aspect of the town, with its broad and grass-covered street, give it a peculiar appearance, unlike any other village in the valley. Middle Street was laid out in 1683, and was originally twenty rods in width. It has however been reduced to about eleven rods.

East Street was laid out in 1825. In 1657, Edward Hopkins of Hartford, left a donation of about £400, which was appropriated to establish a school. In 1667, the town granted to the trustees of this fund, a meadow in North Hadley, which now contains about 140 acres. Various other accessions have been made, the Legislature in 1816 granted an act of incorporation, and gave them a quarter of a township of land, situated in what is now the State of Maine. A building was erected in 1814, on the middle lane which runs between East and West streets. From that time Hopkins' Academy became one of the notable institutions in this valley. The old building was burned in 1860, and the school held its sessions in rooms fitted up in the basement of the Congregational Church until 1865, when the fund was incorporated with that raised by the town, and a building erected for a High School. The old Academy can reckon many of the most distinguished men in New England among her graduates.

This town is celebrated as being the place of refuge of "the regicides," William Goffe and Edward Whalley, two of the judges who condemned Charles I. They had both occupied positions in Cromwell's army, the former a major-general and the latter a lieutenant-general. After the restoration of the monarchy, an order for their apprehension as traitors was issued. They made their escape and reached Boston in 1660. They resided in New Haven, Conn., for three years and a half after their arrival, obliged all the while to use their utmost vigilance, frequently being compelled to resort to the woods and caves to elude their pursuers. At one time they secreted themselves under a bridge near New Haven, while the King's officers rode over on horseback. In October, 1664, they came to Hadley and took up their abode with Rev. Mr. Russell, whose house was situated on the east side of West street, directly north of what is now the main road between Northampton and Amherst. Here they remained concealed fifteen or sixteen years. The dangerous secret was known to Peter Tilton and to a Mr. Smith, who lived at the north end of the village. Through Mr. Tilton, who was frequently a member of the general court, Goffe corresponded with his friends. By one of his letters, dated April 2, 1679, it appears that Whalley died some time previous at Mr. Russell's. He was buried in a tomb formed of mason work and covered with hewn stone, just without the cellar wall of the dwelling, where his remains were found by Mr. Gaylord, in 1794, when he built a house on the site where Mr. Russell's stood. There is also a tradition that Goffe died in Hadley, and was buried in the garden or near the house of Mr. Tilton. On the first of September, 1675, while the people were assembled, on a fast day, at the church, the town was attacked by the Indians and thrown into the greatest confusion. A man of venerable aspect and commanding mien, suddenly appeared among them, assumed command, arrayed the men in the best posture for defense, and by his example inspired them with new vigor. As soon as the enemy were repelled the stranger withdrew. Speculation concerning their deliverer was rife, but it only ended in the conjecture that the town had been saved by its guardian angel. The supposed angel was none other than General Goffe.

Here was manufactured, the first broom that was made in this country from broom corn. About 1790 broom corn was introduced into the town, and grown as an ornamental plant. At that time brooms were made of birch. A negro named Ebar commenced to manufacture the brush into brooms, and Levi Dickinson sold them. This was the origin of the broom business, which has now become one of the most important in this vicinity. At first Mr. Dickinson met with much opposition, there being a great prejudice against what was regarded as an innovation. In Hadley alone there are manufactured nearly $200,000 worth of brooms and brushes annually. Formerly all the brush consumed in the town was raised in the valley; now much of it is grown in the West.

Hadley is also the birth place of Maj. Gen. Joseph Hooker, for a time commander of the Army of the Potomac.

AMHERST AND ITS COLLEGES.

Seven miles east of Northampton is Amherst and its colleges. About a mile below, and about the same distance above, Northampton, the town is in full view, lying beyond Hadley and apparently at the base of the eastern range of hills, but really about two miles from them. Amherst College, though one of the youngest in New England, is already in the first rank of educational institutions. The college edifices are ten in number, grouped on the summit of a gentle eminence and commanding an unsurpassed view, of the surrounding country, for miles on every side. Part of the buildings, dating back to the foundation of the college, are old and cannot boast much in the way of architectural beauty; but the most of them are of comparatively recent construction, and besides sustaining that great test of every building, adaptation to the use intended, are really fine edifices in themselves, and ornaments to the town. Among them may be mentioned the Library building, Williston Hall—erected by the munificence of Hon. Samuel Williston, of Easthampton, who has been a liberal patron of the college—the Appleton Cabinet, the Observatory and Octagonal Cabinet, the Gymnasium, and the new Dormitory.

But the greatest pride of Amherst College is the cabinets; and any one who examines them even cursorily, will acknowledge that the pride is a legitimate and just one. On entering the college grounds, the first building that attracts the attention is the Octagonal Cabinet, so-called. The upper room of this building is entirely devoted to Prof. Charles U. Shepard's Mineralogical Cabinet, which comprises 6000 specimens of minerals of the rarest and choicest character and fully arranged and labeled for study. Here is also the largest collection of meteorites in the world, gathered by untiring industry and at great expense by Prof. Shepard. The casual observer, and the man of science will alike love to linger long in this room; the uneducated attracted by the beautiful colors and unusual forms of the minerals, and their beautiful arrangement, and the educated to study the rare and costly specimens here exhibited. To those of a practical turn of mind, it may be interesting to know that the value of the whole collection is almost fabulous, and that single specimens cost thousands of dollars. In the lower room of the same building is the Wood's Geological Cabinet, containing 20,000 specimens of American and foreign rocks and fossils, offering unrivaled facilities for the students of this branch of science. Joined to the Octagonal Cabinet and opening from it, is the Nineveh Gallery, containing relics from Nineveh, and large sculptured slabs, arranged as they stood in the palace of Sardanapalus at Nimroud. Here, also is a collection of coins and medals, and a quantity of Indian relics. On the other side of the cabinet is the observatory, containing all the necessary instruments for taking observations of the celestial bodies. Beyond the chapel, and on a lower terrace, is the Appleton Cabinet, in the upper room of which is the Adams Zoological Cabinet, containing specimens of 5,900 species of animals, and 8,000 species of shell. Here also is an Herbarium containing more than 4,000 species of dried plants, with the seeds and cuttings of tropical plants and trees, besides a private collection of Lichens, consisting of 800 species. The lower room, one hundred and ten feet long, and forty-five feet wide, is devoted entirely to the Ichnological Cabinet, presenting some 9000 examples of tracks in stone. This cabinet peculiarly belongs to Amherst, and more than any other one thing, perhaps, has given a reputation to the College. There is no other cabinet like it in the world, in extent, and very few in kind. The science of Ichnology had its birth at Amherst; here lived its founder, Dr. Hitchcock, and here are gathered its richest specimens, "foot-prints on the sands of time," stone histories of the past. These tracks on the sand-stone of the Connecticut Valley, tell queer legends of the animal life of long ago, and nothing can be more interesting, than to spend an hour or a day in viewing these relics, now scientifically arranged and classified.

The Massachusetts State Agricultural College was located in Amherst, in 1863, about a mile north of the village, and some 400 acres purchased for an experimental farm. The erection of the necessary buildings was commenced in 1866, and the College is now in successful operation, proving all that was hoped for it as an educational institution. Its President, W. S. Clark, is an enthusiast in his vocation and has won great success.

THE GREAT BEND IN THE CONNECTICUT.

Leaving Northampton, a mile north of the town the tourist comes to the great Bend in the Connecticut—the river running seven miles to gain one. The broad meadows, and the village of Hadley, extending across the peninsular, from one bank of the

Connecticut to the other, and the view down the Connecticut and across the meadows, here obtained, present to the beholder a scene of rural beauty rarely met with. It was at this place that the Farmington Canal, from New Haven to Northampton, terminated. The patronage being insufficient, it was abandoned more than thirty years ago. This is the last view had of the Connecticut until the tourist approaches South Vernon, nearly thirty miles

THE GREAT BEND.

distant. The river takes a more circuitous route, bearing further to the east.

HATFIELD.

Hatfield, four miles from Northampton, is a pleasant town, on the west bank of the Connecticut. Its inhabitants are chiefly engaged in agriculture, fattening cattle, and raising tobacco and other farm crops. The village is about two miles east of the depot. This, like many other towns in this region, suffered from attacks of Indians, in its early days. May 30, 1676, some six or seven hundred Indians invaded the town, burnt twelve houses, and killed a number of the inhabitants. A company of twenty-five men, from Hadley, crossed the river, attacked the Indians, and succeeded in killing twenty-five. Another attack was made Sept. 19, 1677, by 800 Indians, who killed eleven whites and carried seventeen into captivity. Oliver Smith, the founder of the Smith Charities, lived in this town, as did also his neice, Miss Sophia Smith, now dead, the founder of the Smith College for women, at Northampton.

WHATELY.

Whately, four miles from Hatfield, is a small agricultural town. The village will be noticed on the hill west of the railroad.

SUGAR-LOAF MOUNTAIN.

Soon after leaving Whately, Sugar-Loaf Mountain will be observed on the right. It is a conical peak of red sandstone, 500 feet above the plain. It stands on the west bank of the Connecticut, within two hundred yards of the river, and rises almost perpendicularly from the meadows below. North of it is another peak, somewhat higher, but seldom visited, as the view is less varied and beautiful. Sugar Loaf stands, as it were, at the head of the valley, and the southern view is remarkable for its beauty. On the left, east of the river, and almost underneath the mountain, is the village of Sunderland, accessible from the west side by a covered toll bridge. South, and on the same side of the river, are the villages of North Amherst, Amherst, Belchertown, North Hadley, and Hadley. On the west side are South Deerfield, Whately, Hatfield, Northampton, and Easthampton. Skirting the southern horizon are the summits of Mounts Holyoke and Tom, and

SUGAR-LOAF MOUNTAIN.

between them, through the gateway to the ocean, glimmering in the sunlight, are seen the church spires in Holyoke and Chicopee. Here lies before you a great basin, divided through its center by the Connecticut, and on either side the numerous villages and well cultivated fields add beauty to the scene. At no other point is one more strongly impressed with the great wealth of the valley. Before you, on either side of the river, are thousands of dwellings and workshops, seemingly almost a continuous village. On this plane, in years gone by, where peace and happiness now dwell, were enacted some terrible and bloody scenes. Here, on this

TABLE ROCK.

very mountain peak, as is supposed, King Philip, the terror of the early settlers, had his headquarters, and from which he kept watch over the movements of the whites below. Near the southern face of the mountain was fought a great battle, and at the right, north of the village of South Deerfield, was enacted one of the most terrible and heart-rending massacres ever perpetrated by Indians. The monument erected to commemorate the event, can be seen in front of the North Church. Table Rock, on the eastern side, is a feature of great interest. It projects from the mountain side, and at a single leap one could strike the plain hundreds of feet below. Underneath Table Rock is King Philip's Chair, cut by the Indians from the solid rock. East of Sugar Loaf, on the opposite side of the Connecticut, is Mount Toby, twelve hundred feet above the river. In the north-west can be seen Shelburne Mountain and Haystack—the latter in Vermont. The Hotel on the summit was built in 1864. Persons wishing to visit the mountain can leave the cars at South Deerfield, a mile and a half from the summit. A road has been constructed to the Hotel. A tower has been built on Mount Toby, on the east side of the river, which can be seen from the cars. From it there is a fine view of the valley.

SOUTH DEERFIELD—THE BATTLE OF BLOODY BROOK.

South Deerfield, a village in the town of Deerfield, at the base of Sugar-Loaf Mountain, is chiefly noted for having been the scene of one of the most terrible Indian massacres recorded on the pages of history. Here was fought the battle of Bloody Brook, the history of which is familiar to every schoolboy in the land. The first conflict between the whites and Indians took place in August, 1675, at the south end of Sugar Loaf, where Captains Lathrop and Beers, who had left Hadley in pursuit of some Indians who were attempting to join King Philip, overtook them. In this engagement twenty-six Indians and ten Whites were killed. On the 18th of September, a force of 80 soldiers, under command of Capt. Lathrop, who had been stationed at Hadley, was returning from Deerfield, acting as a guard to some teams that were transporting grain to Hadley, and while halting at a small stream, north of where the village now stands, an attack was made. The stream was then bordered by trees on which the native grape clustered; and while the men were gathering them, some 700 Indians, probably under command of Philip, fell upon them and most cruelly butchered almost the entire force. Only seven or eight escaped to tell the sad tale. Including Capt. Lathrop and the teamsters, the number killed was about ninety. Capt. Moseley, then at Deerfield, hearing the firing, hurried to the spot, attacked the Indians, and after a most deadly strife, put them to flight. Their loss was about ninety-six warriors. Nearly all the whites who were slain, were buried in one common grave, a short distance south of where the massacre took place. A few years ago, a monument twenty-six feet high was erected to commemorate the sad event. Edward Everett delivered an eloquent address on the occasion of the laying of the corner stone.

DEERFIELD—INDIAN MASSACRES.

Passing Sugar-Loaf Mountain, and the Bloody Brook Monument, you soon come to Old Deerfield. Few towns in New England suffered so much in its earlier days, from Indian depredations, as did this. Within its borders, from King Philip's war to that waged by the French and Indians, nearly 150 white settlers were killed, and many others carried into captivity. About thirty years after the massacre of Captain Lathrop and his men, at Bloody Brook, another, and, if possible, more heart-rending deed was transacted at the village of Deerfield. On the 29th of February, 1704, Maj. Hertel de Rouville, with upwards of 340 French and Indians, arrived at Petty's Plain, north of Deerfield meadows, which the tourist will notice toward the north-west previous to crossing the bridge over Deerfield river. Here he halted until the next morning, when he moved upon the village of Deerfield. The snow having drifted to the top of the palisades, which had been constructed as a defense, the entire force entered the fortifications undiscovered, the settlers being in a profound sleep. The houses were broken open, the frightened and defenseless inhabitants dragged from their beds, and such as offered resistance were killed, and the others taken prisoners. Only a few, escaped. Rev. John Williams, the minister of the town, was awakened from his sleep and rushed to the door and found the enemy entering. Calling the two soldiers, who lodged in the house, he sprang back and seized a pistol and attempted to fire at an Indian. It missing fire, he was seized and bound. Two of his children and a negro woman were taken to the door and butchered. Mr. Williams was kept standing in the cold for an hour before being permitted to dress. His savage captors, meantime, amused themselves by threatening his life and swinging their hatchets over his head. Mrs. Williams had recently given birth to a child, and still in a feeble condition, was compelled to dress, and herself and five children taken captives. An attack was made on the house of John Sheldon, which they found hard to enter. An attempt was made by the Indians to split the door down with their hatchets. Finally it was partly opened and a musket thrust in and fired. Mrs. Sheldon, who had risen and was dressing, was hit and killed. The house was used as a place of confinement for the prisoners until all were gathered in from the other parts of the village. One house was defended by seven men, for whom the women cast bullets while the fight was in progress. When the sun was about an hour high, after the houses had been plundered, and many of them set on fire, Rouville and his men started for Canada, halting at Petty's Plain, where they had left their packs and snow-shoes a few hours before. Capt. Stoddard escaped from Mr. Williams' house during the attack, by leaping from the window. He tore up a cloak, which he had hurriedly seized, and bound about his feet, and ran to Hatfield. A son of Capt. Sheldon escaped the same way, and also went to Hatfield. A force left Hatfield in pursuit of the Indians, and they were overtaken north of Deerfield, where a skirmish ensued, but the pursuers being much the smaller party, were obliged to retreat—not, however, until they had lost nine of their number. The captives taken by Rouville numbered 180, and the killed 47. The enemy's loss exceeded 40. Mrs. Williams, who had become weak and exhausted on the second day's march, was thrown down by the water while crossing a rapid stream, and her savage captor, thinking it impossible for her to continue the march, buried his tomahawk in her forehead, which soon caused her death. Mr. Williams was much of the time separated from his wife, and was in advance when she was cruelly butchered. She was the daughter of Rev. Eleazer Mather, the first minister of Northampton, and was an educated, refined, and noble woman. At White River, Rouville divided his forces—one party going up that river to Canada, and another up the Connecticut. Mr. Williams' party followed the White River route, and most of his children the other, and they barely escaped death from famine. After arriving in Canada, the French treated Mr. Williams with great kindness, and finally he was redeemed by Gov. Vaudreuil. In 1706 Mr. Williams and four of his children, with other captives to the number of fifty seven, embarked on board of a ship at Quebec, sent there by Gov. Dudley, and sailed for Boston. His daughter, Eunice, seven years old when captured, he was unable to procure, and she remained with the Indians. Arriving at womanhood she married an Indian, and by him had a family of children. From her descended Rev. Eleazer Williams, late missionary to the Indians at Green Bay, Wisconsin, the pretended

Dauphin of France. A few years after the war she visited Deerfield with her husband, and a number of other Indians. She was dressed in Indian costume, and all inducements offered her to remain were unavailing. A brother, who was taken to Canada with her, became the first pastor in Longmeadow. She subsequently twice visited him, but she could not be prevailed upon to remain, on the ground that it would endanger her soul, having become a convert to Romanism. Mr. Williams, after his release from captivity, resumed his ministerial labors at Deerfield. His wife, who was killed on the way to Canada, was brought back to Deerfield, and her remains now lie interred by the side of her husband. Lossing states that one of the motives which led to the attack on Deerfield, was to recover a bell, that had been sent from France to a Catholic church in St. Regis, on the St. Lawrence, and which was captured by an English vessel, while on the way, and sent to Salem and thence to Mr. Williams' church at Deerfield. The bell was carried off by the Indians and buried near where the village of Burlington is now situated, receiving the benedictions of the Catholic priest, who accompanied the expedition. In the spring it was taken to St. Regis, and is still in use at the Catholic Cathedral at that place. The "Old Indian House," known to former visitors and residents of Deerfield, showing the marks of the tomahawks upon the door, and perforations made by the balls inside, was the one in which Mrs. Sheldon was killed, and where the captives were temporarily confined. It was taken down a few years ago, but the door has been preserved, and is now in the Pocumtuck Hotel.

Quite a number of distinguished men have been natives of Deerfield; among whom may be mentioned Gen. Epaphras Hoyt, author of Antiquarian Researches, the late President Edward Hitchcock, of Amherst College, and Maj. Gen. Rufus Saxton. The Deerfield Academy, still in exsistence, was formerly one of the most noted educational institutions in the country.

DEERFIELD BRIDGE.

Leaving Deerfield, you soon come to the bridge over the Deerfield River. It is 750 feet in length, and from 48 to 90 feet above the water. It was burnt on the morning of July 17, 1864, and before night half a dozen saw mills were employed sawing out lumber to be used in rebuilding it. Within three weeks the lumber was all on the ground, and within six weeks trains were able to cross the bridge.

THE DEERFIELD BRIDGE.

GREENFIELD.

New York, 172; White Mountains, 148; Lake Memphremagog, 193; Montreal, 274; Quebec, 354 miles.

GREENFIELD, another of the many beautiful towns seen ont his route, is the next, and an important station for its railroad connections. It has a population of about 4,000, and is a thriving and prosperous town—the legal and commercial center of a large number of prosperous rural villages. Its streets are wide, and lined on either side by old and magnificent elms. It has long been a favorite stopping place for summer visitors, and in and about the town are some charming views of natural scenery. Its drives are numerous and pleasant, adding greatly to the interest of the town. After crossing the Deerfield River, over the Cheapside bridge, the track of the Vermont and Massachusetts Railroad will be seen on the right. At this place it curves to the east and follows the valley of the Deerfield River to the Connecticut, and then to Fitchburg, where it connects with the road to Boston. At this point, also, but to the left, will be observed the railroad track leading to the famous Hoosic Tunnel. Parties desirous of visiting the tunnel will here change cars, and, crossing Green River over the "skeleton bridge," proceed westward along the Deerfield River, to the eastern end of the tunnel, where they can enter and examine it at their leisure.

"I'M NOT GOING ON THIS TRAIN."

A lady took the cars, one morning, that, as she supposed, were going to Springfield; but she soon learned her mistake, as they moved away from the depot in the opposite direction. Hurrying to the platform, she commenced shouting, in a loud tone of voice, at the same time vigorously flourishing her umbrella: "I am *not* going on *this* train! I *am not* going on *this* train! I tell you I am *not going on this train!*" But she did, to the great amusement of the crowd of people at the depot.

TURNER'S FALLS.

Some three or four miles east of Greenfield are Turner's Falls, in the Connecticut. Here the river makes a descent of 70 feet in two and one-half miles, and a company has here purchased 700 acres of land, and have built up quite an important manufacturing village. A branch railroad connects this village with the Vermont and Massachusetts Railroad and Greenfield.

During King Philip's war, a force, headed by Capt. Turner, marched to this place and attacked the Indians, who had gathered at the falls for the purpose of fishing. Three hundred were killed or drowned, and Capt. Turner, himself, was shot during the latter part of the day. The bird tracks of the Connecticut Valley, which are of so much interest to scientific men, were first found here.

BERNARDSTON.

Bernardston, seven miles from Greenfield, is a small village of several hundred inhabitants. Here is located Powers' Institute, an educational institution of some note. This place was also the residence of the late Lieut. Gov. Cushman, a gentleman of wealth and refinement, who did much to elevate and beautify the village in which he resided, and, at his death, left means to fully supply with books a public library previously founded by himself. He also left other legacies for public purposes, among which was a considerable fund to the town, provided it would change its corporate name to Cushman. A proviso accompanies this bequest that, in case the town failed to change its name within a certain time, then, any new town, created within a specified time might claim the fund on the adoption of his name. In case it is not thus disposed of, at the expiration of a certain number of years, then any town in Massachusetts, of not less than 1000 inhabitants may take the name of Cushman—and the money.

After leaving the station, going north, the church spire in Gill can be seen, several miles eastward. The railroad curves to the east, coming out upon the plateau above the Connecticut, where the first view of the river is had since leaving Northampton.

NORTHFIELD.

Before reaching South Vernon, the village of Northfield will be seen on the opposite side of the Connecticut. A branch of the Vermont and Massachusetts Railroad passes through the town, and the bridge over the Connecticut will be noticed northwest of the village. In the early part of September, 1675, the town was attacked by Indians, ten persons killed, and the other settlers driven to the fort. Shortly after the pursuit and attack on the Indians, south of Sugar-Loaf Mountain, Capt. Beers was dispatched from Hadley—the headquarters of the English forces—to take provisions to the settlers at Northfield. Within two miles of the fort they were surprised, and Capt. Beers mortally wounded. The men saved themselves the best way they could, but out of a force of 37 men, only 16 returned to Hadley.

SOUTH VERNON—THE STATE LINE.

At this place, the traveler leaves Massachusetts and enters Vermont. The boundary line between the two states passes through the southern end of the passenger station house. Here the Vermont and Massachusetts Railroad, which intersects the eastern and western line at Grout's Corner, forms a junction with the other roads, and extends to Brattleboro. This branch of the Vermont and Massachusetts Railroad, and the New London Northern, which terminates at Grout's, are operated, under a lease, by the Central Vermont, which runs trains from Brattleboro to New London. The Ashuelot Railroad, extending to Keene, N. H., twenty-three miles distant, connects here with the main line.

Leaving South Vernon, the tourist is soon riding along upon the banks of the Connecticut, charmed with the beautiful scenery before him,—the extended view up the valley, with the mountain range opposite Brattleboro in the distance, and the beautiful island, covered with forest trees, in the Connecticut, in the foreground.

MONADNOCK MOUNTAIN.

Just as the train approaches Vernon station, the summit of Monadnock, thirty miles eastward, in Jaffrey, N. H., can be seen through the valley of the Ashuelot. It is 3,450 feet above the sea, and is the first land seen by sailors entering Boston harbor. In clear weather Bunker Hill Monument can be seen with the aid of the glass. From the summit forty lakes and a large number of villages are in full view, and the scenery around the mountain is grand and beautiful. A hotel has been erected half way to the summit. To reach it, from the Connecticut

Valley, the tourist should leave the train at South Vernon, proceed to Keene by the Ashuelot Railroad, and thence to Troy on the Cheshire Railroad, from which place a stage runs to the hotel, five miles distant. Boston people can leave the city by the early morning train, visit the mountain and return home the same day.

VERNON.—CAPTURE OF MRS. HOWE BY THE INDIANS.

In the early settlement of Vermont, Forts Bridgman and Sartwell, built to protect the inhabitants from the Indians, were the scenes of bloody massacres. The former was attacked and destroyed June 24, 1746, and on July 27, 1755, the latter was entered and its occupants carried into captivity. These forts stood west of the railroad, nearly a mile north of the depot. Among those captured were Mrs. Jemima Howe and her seven children. Her husband, Caleb Howe, had been previously killed in the field while returning from work. Mrs. Howe's youngest child was torn from her breast, and it perished with hunger. Herself and other children, after a long march, reached Canada. She spent a number of years there, but by her heroism she procured her release, and with five children returned to Vernon. Her oldest daughter was taken to France, and marrying a Frenchman, never returned to America. Mrs. Howe had been twice married, and both husbands had been killled by Indians. After her return she married a third time, Amos Tute. A son by this husband, Jonathan Tute, died from the effects of inoculation, and was buried in the cemetery in Vernon. Rev. Bunker Gay, of Hinsdale, N. H., more noted for eccentricity than education, wrote an epitaph, which is still legible upon the tombstone, that has caused many a stranger to pause before Jonathan's grave and contemplate his unfortunate end. A few of the more remarkable lines are copied below:

> "Here lies cut down, like unripe fruit,
> A son of Mr. Amos Tute.
> * * * * *
> "To death he fell a helpless prey,
> On April V and Twentieth Day,
> In Seventeen Hundred Seventy-Seven,
> Quitting this world, we hope, for Heaven.
> "Behold the amazing alteration,
> Effected by inoculation;
> The means empowered his life to save,
> Hurried him headlong to the grave."

FORT DUMMER.—FIRST SETTLEMENT IN VERMONT.

Leaving Vernon, you soon come to Fort Dummer, a mile south of the village of Brattleboro, where the first settlement in Vermont was made, and here was born the first white child in the State, John Sargent, whose descendants still reside in Brattleboro. Fort Dummer was built in 1724, by the Colonial authorities of Massachusetts, and named in honor of Sir William Dummer, then Lieut. Governor. The site of the fort was near the river, where a dwelling house now stands, directly east of the large farm house which can be seen near the wooded hills west of the railroad. When the fort was built it was supposed to be within the limits of Massachusetts, and at that time was the northern outpost of civilization.

BRATTLEBORO.

New York, 194; White Mountains, 126; Lake Memphremagog, 171; Montreal, 252; Quebec, 332 miles.

BRATTLEBORO stands in the front rank of the many beautiful towns on the banks of the Connecticut, and none present more attractions to the summer tourist. Situated on an uneven surface, and surrounded by hills and mountains, the scenery is grand and picturesque, and, it is said, bears a striking resemblance to that of Switzerland. The view from Cemetery Hill, a high point just south of the town, is particularly fine. From it is seen the Connecticut on the right, sweeping around the base of Wantastiquet Mountain in a graceful curve, while the mountain itself, rises abruptly from the east bank of the river to the hight of nearly 1,100 feet. To the north and west lies the village, nestling among the shade trees, while further in the distance are numberless hill-tops, outlined on the deep blue sky beyond. Main street extends north and south, parallel with the river, and is one hundred feet above it. Further west are terraces upon which are situated many of the private dwellings. The highest point in the village is nearly three hund-

BRATTLEBORO FROM PROSPECT HILL.

red feet above the river. A mile north of the village is West River, which rises among the Green Mountains, and flows into the Connecticut. In the southern part of the village is Whetstone Brook, which furnishes power for the various manufactories along its banks. Here in Brattleboro, in 1845, was established by Dr. Robert Wesselhœft, a distinguished German, the third Water-Cure in this country, and which for a long time received extensive patronage, some of the most eminent men in the country coming here for treatment. The drives in and around the village are remarkable, winding along the banks of impetuous little streamlets, through beautiful groves, and over high hills. A new drive can be taken every day for nearly a month, without going outside of a radius of four miles, and all of them have peculiar features of interest.

Brattleboro is, or has been, the home of some quite distinguished people. Ex-Governor Holbrook, Governor of Vermont during the first two years of the Rebellion, Gen. J. W. Phelps, a graduate of West Point, a participator in the Florida, Mexican, and Utah wars, and in the Rebellion, serving in the latter with Gen. Butler, in the Department of the Gulf, Charles C. Frost, a distinguished Botanist, and Jacob Estey, the well known head of the Estey Organ Works, the largest in the world, are still residents of the place, while Larkin G. Mead, the Vermont Sculptor, and James Fisk, Jr., spent their youthful days and grew to manhood here. Gen. Phelps is a sturdy old Puritan, entertaining and instructive in conversation, and firmly adhering to the virtue, simplicity and integrity of the early settlers of the country, is a marked character of the town. Opposite the Brooks House is the modest sign, "C. C.

MAIN STREET, LOOKING SOUTH.

Frost, Boot and Shoe Maker." Mr. Frost is one of the most learned in the natural sciences in the country. He has discovered new plants, mastered several languages, and added not a little to the general information, all of which has been done while conducting the business of a shoe store. His books and his business are closely allied. The old rocking chair, which stands back of the stove, and the many volumes that lie within easy reach upon the counter, tell of his studious habits, and how he has employed his time while waiting for customers. He is the oracle of the town, on all that is mysterious in nature, and when any new discovery is made, it is submitted to him for explanation. Not a few times have the villagers gathered about his shop with some rare and remarkable specimen, fully confident that this time "we have a poser for Uncle Charles;" but thus far he has not been found wanting. His services and his devotion to science, have been recognized by several learned societies, which have conferred honors upon him. Mr. Mead, the well known sculptor, earned his first honors here. When a lad, he modeled a statue in snow in the last night of the year, at the head of Main Street, and when the people went forth to their labor New Year's morning, they beheld the "Recording Angel," with tablet in hand, apparently in the act of recording the events of the opening year. This first attempt at sculpture gained him notoriety at once, and his first patron was the late Nicholas Longworth, the Cincinnati millionaire. Subsequently the State gave him a commission to execute in marble, a full length statue of Ethan Allen, now in the vestibule of the State House at Montpelier, and which was made in Brattleboro. It was eminently fitting, as well as quite poetical, that Vermont should give a commission to a gifted son to perpetuate the outward semblance of her greatest hero, in her greatest product—marble. Since then he has resided mostly in Italy, and has achieved a worldwide fame. The monument to Abraham Lincoln, designed by him, and now building at Springfield, Ill., is among his largest and best works.

James Fisk, Jr., came here to reside, when a mere lad; here he commenced his first business operations, going out into the world as a peddler, and achieving great success, he reached out for larger fields in which to operate. He entered them and gained distinction, and at last met a tragic end. He was brought home and laid in the beautiful cemetery south of the depot, which overlooks the town and the magnificent scenery, on a bright winter's day, just as the shadows began to lengthen and overspread the valley below. His generous impulses and his sad death, had touched every heart, and when he was lowered into his last resting place, not a dry eye turned from the impressive scene. Slowly and sadly the large funeral cortege, composed of rich and poor, the residents of the town, and the dwellers in distant cities, turned homeward full of genuine sorrow. His grave is upon the edge of the steep hill which overlooks the valley, and here his wife has erected a beautiful monument, the work of Larkin G. Mead. It stands twenty feet high in the center of the lot, and directly over the remains; on two sides, placed in each corner, are speaking, life-sized female figures, that on the south-west corner representing Music, the right hand resting on an Æolian harp and the left holding a wreath, the head being encircled with laurel. The north-west corner bears the impersonation of railroads, and the other-

MONUMENT TO JAMES FISK, JR.

wise obscure thought of the figure is made plain by the word "railroad" carved upon a book upon which the right hand rests, the head being capped with a crown whose front is an engine; the steamboat is interpreted in a like manner on the south-east corner, the feet encased in sandles, and a miniature steamboat making the front of a crown of flowers; on the north-west corner and completing the group is Commerce, bearing in her right hand a bag of coin, the left holding a rod and the head sustaining a wreath, in the front of which is an eagle. On the north and front side, embedded in the die, is an oval marble medallion, bearing a fine bust of Fisk in relief; just below this in the second base is the raised inscription: "Col. James Fisk, Jr., born April 1, 1831, died Jan. 7, 1872." The marble base of the structure is six feet eight inches by four feet and two inches; the bottom of the cap on which rests the shaft, somewhat over 10 feet in hight, is paneled work, each corner bearing a shield, the whole being engirded with a wreath, while lesser wreaths are put in the center of the four sides; on the shaft is a delicately carved chaplet of flowers and grasses, represented as tied with ribbons. This is one of the most beautiful monuments in New England. It cost about $25,000, and was paid for with the proceeds of Col. Fisk's life insurance.

The Vermont Asylum for the Insane is located in the north part of the town, and is said to be one of the best conducted institutions, of the kind, in the country. It was founded in 1834, by Mrs. Anna Marsh, of Hinsdale, N. H., who died leaving by will, $10,000 for that purpose. The Asylum was incorporated, and is managed by a board of trustees, in accordance with the provisions of the will.

The State of Vermont has contributed, at various times, $23,000 to assist in establishing the institution, and rebuilding the main edifice, which was destroyed by fire in 1862. The Asylum owns 600 acres of land in one body, adjoining the grounds on which the buildings are located, and about as many more of woodland. The labor on the farm is mostly done, voluntarily, by the patients, who are greatly benefited by it.

THE ESTEY ORGAN WORKS.

This is the largest Organ Manufactory in the world. It occupies eight large buildings, and gives employment to five hundred hands. Its successful founder is Mr. Jacob Estey, a gentleman of rare business and social qualities.

The manufacture of reed musical instruments dates back to 1846, at Brattleboro, and like many other now great enterprises, it had a very humble beginning, and but little success until Mr. Estey became its active manager. He was first assisted by Mr. Greene. Their factory was burned in 1857, but was soon rebuilt. In 1861 Mr. Greene withdrew from the firm. Three years later, in 1864, Mr. Estey's manufactory was again burned, with heavy loss, but he again rebuilt, and a year later took in two partners, under the firm name of J. Estey & Co. The business was continued under this management for about fifteen months, and these two partners then retired, and their places were filled by Mr. Levi K. Fuller, a son-in-law of Mr. Estey, and Mr. Julius J. Estey, his son. Mr. Fuller had been in the shops

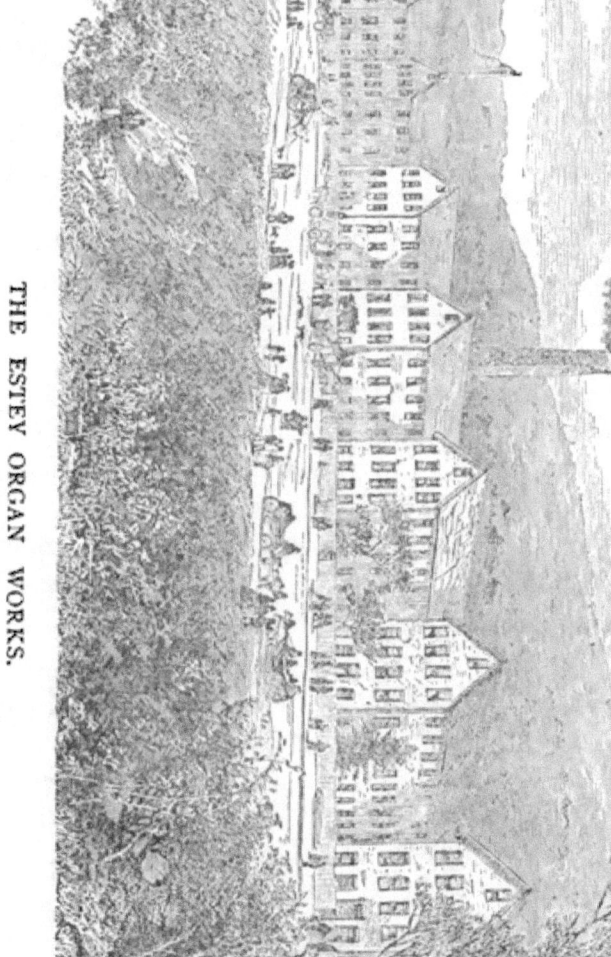

THE ESTEY ORGAN WORKS.

for seven years before, and had thoroughly mastered the mechanical details of the business, and the younger Mr. Estey had been his father's assistant in the business management of the concern. After the second fire, in 1864, the manufactory was located upon the "flats," but the disastrous effects of the freshets, in that locality, admonished them that another location must be sought for the growth and enlargement of their business. A farm of some sixty or seventy acres, fronting on Birge street, and overlooking the village, was selected as a suitable site for the erection of the needed buildings, in 1869, and the firm now has, beyond question, the most convenient, complete, and extensive Reed Organ manufactory in the world. There are eight three-story factories, one hundred feet long, and from thirty to thirty-eight feet in width, all built the same distance from Birge street, upon which they front, and forty feet from each other. A walk at the rear of the second-story connects all these buildings, and, by the aid of this, and by elevators in each building, the transportation of articles from the different buildings, and from the different stories of the same building, is very readily accomplished. A three-hundred horse-power engine furnishes the motive power, and three million feet of lumber are used annually in the business. The present production of organs is two hundred a week, and even this large production does not keep pace with the demand. The sales are all made at wholesale, to local agents, in different parts of the country, and the weekly orders of these agents are constantly ahead of the production. The estimation in which the public holds the Estey Organs is sufficiently attested by the constantly increasing demand for their instruments,—by the unsolicited testimonials of those who have used them, and by some hundred and fifty medals, first premiums, and diplomas, which have been awarded them at fairs and exhibitions in different parts of the country. The capital invested amounts to over a million dollars, and the expenditures for labor reach nearly $300,000 a year. The instruments of this concern stand at the head, and deserve all that is claimed for them. Brattleboro feels justly proud of Mr. Estey, and what he has accomplished, and as he is a true representative of Vermont in sagacity and worth, the people could do no more fitting act than to place him at some future day in the gubernatorial chair.

DISCOVERY OF AN ELEPHANT'S TUSK.

In 1865 a workman, while digging muck on a farm in Brattleboro, found, about five feet below the surface, a part of the tusk of an elephant, forty-four inches in length, eighteen in circumference at the largest, and eleven at the smallest end. It was in a fair state of preservation, and was taken to Montpelier and placed in the historical rooms at the State House. It belonged to a species of elephant long since extinct, that inhabited the northern part of North America, having wandered across the Siberian plains to the Arctic Ocean and Behring

Strait, and beyond, to this country, south, to about the parallel of 40 degrees. Their bones show them to have been about twice the weight, and one-third taller than the modern species. The tusk teeth, and some bones of one of these elephants were found in a muck bed at the summit of the Green Mountains, in Mount Holly, in 1848, by workmen who were building the railroad from Bellows Falls to Rutland.

WANTASTIQUET AND MINE MOUNTAINS.

Opposite Brattleboro, on the east side of the Connecticut, are Wantastiquet and Mine Mountains, the former rising from the river to the hight of 1,061 feet. The latter extends eastward from Wantastiquet, and is only separated from it by a narrow gorge. During the latter part of the last century, a party sunk a shaft many feet into the solid rock on Mine Mountain, in search of silver, which they had incredulously been led to believe existed there, but after the expenditure of large sums of money, the enterprise was abandoned.

The Cemetery, south of the depot, and its charming views, and the view from the Park, in the north part of the village, are points that are easily reached, and should not be missed by those visiting Brattleboro. Of the many drives, that to the Bliss farm, two miles north of the Hotel, is the finest. The view is unsurpassed in grandeur and beauty.

BROOKS HOUSE, BRATTLEBORO, VT.

In 1870, the west side of Main street was nearly all burned, and since, it has been substantially rebuilt. Mr. George J. Brooks, a native of the town, for a long time a resident of California, erected a handsome building for a Hotel, which is now known as the Brooks House. It is the largest, and one of

BROOKS HOUSE, BRATTLEBORO.

best hotels in the Connecticut Valley. Its rooms are large and pleasant, and the appointments of the house, in every part, are complete. Its landlord, Chas. G. Lawrence, is one of the best in the country, and his guests are sure of receiving the best of attention. For a summer residence, Brattleboro and the Brooks House are unsurpassed. A good livery stable is connected with the hotel.

"WERE YOU SUCCESSFUL?"

An old lady took the early train for Springfield, and as Conductor Hare came around to collect the tickets, she reached into her pocket and drew forth a fine tooth comb, and handed it to him, supposing it to be her ticket. He held it up a moment remarking as he did so: "Madam, we are not taking these here now. I used that before I left home." Seeing the mistake that had been made, she replied, "Ah, indeed. Were you successful?"

WEST RIVER.—GEN. STARK.

Leaving Brattleboro, the railroad continues along the bank of the Connecticut, and, for some distance, the mountain scenery on the opposite side, is exceedingly beautiful. About a mile north of the village you cross West River on a bridge at its mouth. Its Indian name is Wantastiquet, signifying straight or arrowy. It rises among the Green Mountains, about thirty miles west of Brattleboro, and is a very rapid stream.

A little way north of West River, near the dwelling seen on the opposite side, Gen. Stark crossed the Connecticut, with an Aid, on his way from Manchester, to fight the battle of Bennington. The gallant General was taken across the river by the ferryman, in a little old canoe. He hurried forward to Bennington, where he afterward achieved a great victory over the invaders of our country.

DUMMERSTON, PUTNEY, AND EAST PUTNEY.

Continuing north, the small stations of Dummerston, Putney, and East Putney are passed. Just north of Putney, the village will be seen west of the railroad. Opposite East Putney is the village of Westmoreland, in New Hampshire, one of the churches standing upon the hill north-west of the village. Above the church can be seen the track of the Cheshire railroad, curving eastward.

WESTMINSTER—FIRST BLOOD OF THE REVOLUTION.

About twenty miles from Brattleboro and four from Bellows Falls, is Westminster. This is a place of great historic interest, as here begun the opening scenes of the American Revolution. A bitter quarrel had sprung up between the royal authorities in New York and the people who had purchased land in Vermont, under the New Hampshire grants —the latter not wishing to acknowledge the illegitimacy of the authority under which they held their titles. It was finally determined that the New York royal court should not hold its approaching session at Westminister, and after trying to dissuade the judge from holding the court, who gave some equivocal promises, the people, unarmed, seized the court house, on the afternoon of the day that the court was to be held. The royal authorities, not liking to be put down by what they considered a mob, attempted to enforce their rights by arms. At eleven o'clock at night, while the people of Westminster had possession of the court house, the royal authorities fired into it, mortally wounding William French and Daniel Houghton. This occurred March 13th, 1775. French was only 22 years of age, and was a resident of Brattleboro. Previous to the attack on the court house, he went from Brattleboro to Dummerston, where he joined the Dummerston Rangers. He was buried in Westminster, and the grave is still seen in the village cemetery. The original grave stone is in existence, and is kept in the old church. The court house stood at the top of the hill in the highway, about a mile south of the depot. The principal men of the royalist party were seized and carried, under escort of Col. Benjamin Fellows, the founder of Walpole, to Northampton, Mass., and lodged in jail. The New York authorities, however, afterwards procured their release. It is claimed that the Westminster massacre so enraged Gen. Gage, at Boston, the British commander, showing, as he thought, the determined spirit of the people to resist British authority, that he was induced to march to Lexington, and inflict the blow which opened the Revolution. If so, Westminster is entitled to the honor of being the birthplace of American liberty. The oldest church in Vermont is now standing in Westminster, and can be seen from the cars—the only one in the village having a spire. It was erected in 1770. It is now used as a shop and town hall. The legislature of Vermont held some of its first sessions in the town, and the first printing office in the State was established here in 1778, and the first paper, the Vermont Gazette, in 1781. The village lies about a mile south of the depot, upon broad table land, and is very pleasantly situated.

WALPOLE—THE HOME OF THE BELLOWS FAMILY.

Opposite Westminster, lying above the river, is the pleasant village of Walpole, one of the prettiest and neatest in the valley of the Connecticut. The streets are wide, and the dwellings large and elegant. There is little business in the town, and it is chiefly noted as the home of the Bellows family, descendants of Col. Benjamin Bellows, the founder of the town, who came here from Lunenburg, Mass., more than a hundred years ago. The members of the family, who have been abroad and secured wealth, have usually come back to the old home to spend the remainder of their days. Among those who have summer residences here is Rev. Dr. Henry W. Bellows, of New York, a great grandson of the founder of the town. His cottage can be seen just south of the village, near a large brick dwelling. The descendants, who wished to honor their distinguished ancestor, gathered from all parts of the country, in 1854, and erected a marble monument, in the village cemetery, to his memory. An address was delivered by Rev. Dr. Bellows, giving an account of the early settlement of the place. Col. Bellows received a grant of the township of Gov. Wentworth, and came to Walpole in 1752, where he built a fort upon an impregnable point, overlooking the Connecticut, a mile north of the village, near the house now owned by Thomas Bellows. He organized a town government, and seems to have been moderator, town clerk, and selectman—all in one. He was a marked man, and rendered great service in enlisting and equipping men for the Revolution. Before Col. Bellows built his mill, he was obliged to carry his corn to Northampton, Mass., to have it ground, going down in boats in the Spring, and returning with meal and other stores. Within the last few years Walpole has become quite a place of resort during the summer, and there is a large boarding house on the hill, and a hotel in the village, where good accommodations are provided. Travelers who have been abroad state that the scenery around Walpole bears a striking resemblance to that around Berne, in Switzerland. From Derry Hill can be seen Saddleback, Monadnock, Ascutney, and the whole Green Mountain range. Blanchard and Ravine Falls, near the village, have many admirers among those stopping in the town.

AN INDIAN ATTACK.—HEROISM OF JOHN KILBURN.

John Kilburn was another of the early settlers of Walpole. When Col. Bellows came to the town, he found Kilburn in a garrisoned house, near Cold River, about two miles north of Walpole. In the summer of 1775, two men were shot by Indians. "Shortly before this," says Dr. Bellows in his address, "an Indian, by the name of Philip, had visited Kilburn's house, in a friendly manner, pretending to be in want of provisions. He was supplied with flints and flour and dismissed. It was ascertained, that this same Indian had visited all the settlements on the river, doubtless to procure information of the state of their defense. Word came from Governor Shirly, that 500 Indians were collecting in Canada, whose aim was the butchery and extinction of the whole white population on the river.

Col. Benj. Bellows had at this time about 30 men at his fort, about half a mile south of Kilburn's.

but too distant to afford him any aid. About noon on the 17th day of August, 1755, Kilburn and his son John, in his eighteenth year, and a man by the name of Peak and his son, were returning home to dinner from the field, when one of them discovered the red legs of the Indians among the alders, 'as thick as grasshoppers.' They instantly made for the house, fastened the doors and prepared for an obstinate defense. Kilburn's wife Ruth, and his daughter Hetty, were already in the house. In about fifteen minutes, the savages were seen crawling up the bank east of the house, and as they crossed a foot path, one by one, 197 were counted; about the same number it afterward proved had remained in ambush, near the mouth of Cold River, but soon joined the attacking party.

The savages appeared to have learned that Col. Bellows and his men were at work at his mill, about a mile east, on what is now called the Blanchard Brook, near where it is crossed by the Drewsville road, and they intended to waylay and murder them before attacking Kilburn's house. Col. Bellows and his men were now returning home, each with a bag of meal on his back, when the dogs began to growl and betray the neighborhood of an enemy. The Colonel, knowing the language of the dogs, and the wiles of the Indians, instantly adopted his policy. He directed his men, throwing off the meal, to crawl carefully to the rise of the land, and on reaching the top of the bank to spring together to their feet, give one whoop and instantly drop into the sweet fern. The movement had the desired effect to draw the Indians from their ambush. At the sound of the whoop, fancying themselves discovered, the whole body of savages rose from the bushes in a semi-circle, round the path Col. Bellows was to have followed. His men fired upon the Indians, and they were so disconcerted, that they darted into the bushes and disappeared. The Colonel, sensible of his unequal force, hurried his men off by the shortest cut to the fort, and prepared for its defense.

The Indians then determined to take vengeance upon a weaker party, and soon appeared on the eminence east of Kilburn's house. Here the same treacherous Philip, who had visited him and partaken of his hospitality so short a time before, came forward under the shelter of a tree, and summoned the little garrison to surrender. 'Old John, Young John,' was his cry, 'I know ye, come out here. We give you good quarter.' 'Quarter!' vociferated old Kilburn, in a voice of thunder, 'You black rascal, begone, or we'll quarter you.' It was a brave reply for four men to make to four hundred! Philip returned, and after a short consultation, the war-whoop rang out, as if, to use the language of on ear-witness, 'all the devils in hell had been let loose.' Kilburn, lucky and prudent enough to get the first fire, before the smoke of the battle perplexed his aim, was confident he saw Philip fall. The fire from the little garrison was returned by a shower of balls from the savages, who rushed forward to the attack. The roof next to the eminence from which the attack was made, was a perfect "riddle-sieve.' Some of the Indians fell at once to butchering the cattle; others to a wanton destruction of the grain, while the larger part kept up an incessant fire at the house. Meanwhile Kilburn and his men —aye, his women—were all busily at work. Their powder they poured into their hats for greater convenience; the women loaded the guns, of which they had several spare ones—all of them being kept hot by incessant use. As their stock of lead grew short, they suspended blankets over their heads to catch the balls of the enemy, which penetrated one side of the roof and fell short of the other. These were immediately run by these Spartan women into bullets, and before they had time to cool, were sent back to the enemy from whom they came. Several attempts were made to force the door, but the unerring aim of the marksmen within sent such certain death to the assailants, that they soon desisted from their efforts. Most of the time the Indians kept behind logs and stumps, and avoided as best they could, the fire of the little Gibralter. The whole afternoon, even till sundown, the battle continued, until, as the sun set, the savages unable to conquer so small a fortress, discouraged and baffled, forsook the ground, and as was supposed, returned to Canada, abandoning the expedition, on which they had set out. It is not unreasonable to suppose, that their fatal experience here, through the matchless defense of those Walpole heroes and heroines, was instrumental in saving hundreds of the dwellers on the frontier from the horrors of an Indian massacre. Seldom did it fall to the lot of early settlers to win a more brilliant crown, than John Kilburn earned in this glorious exploit. Peak got the only wound of his party, receiving a ball in the hip, from exposure at a port-hole, which unhappily, for lack of surgical care, caused his death on the fifth day. The Indians never again appeared in Walpole, although the war did not terminate until eight years afterward. John Kilburn lived to see his fourth generation on the stage, and enjoy the benefits of a high civilization, on the spot he had rescued from the savages. A plane stone in Walpole burying ground commemorates his departure, and speaks his eulogy in a brief, expressive phrase. His son John last visited the scenes of his youthful exploits in 1814, and died at Shrewsbury, Vt., in 1822. What amount of destruction Kilburn made among the savages, it was impossible to tell, as they carefully carried off and concealed their dead."

MOUNT KILBURN.—THE GOVERNOR'S CALF PASTURE.

Opposite Bellows Falls village, in New Hampshire, is Mt. Kilburn, formerly known as Fall Mountain. It is a little over 800 feet high, and from the summit, a fine view of the village and the distant mountain peaks is had. The early settlers gave it the name of Fall Mountain, from the fact that at its base are the Great Falls in the Connecticut. In 1856 President Hitchcock and the Students of Amherst and Middlebury Colleges, met at Bellows Falls and christened it Mt. Kilburn, in honor of the hero, who fought so gallantly from his little fort, just below the south end of the mountain. This mountain is situated in Walpole, and was included in the grant to Col. Benj. Bellows, the founder of the town. Quite an amusing anecdote is related concerning it: "Gov. Wentworth, in his grants of land, reserved 500 acres in each township, and in making his selection in Walpole, consulted Col. Bellows, as to what was the most favorable portion to lay claim to —expressing his own decided preference for 500 acres in the immediate neighborhood of the Great Falls as the probable site of the future settlement. The Colonel very honestly told him that the land thereabout would make a very good calf pasture, but nothing better. The Governor, perhaps, imagining that the Colonel wished to appropriate these lands to himself, and so discourage his own selection of them, at once resolved to lay his claim there, and his 500 acres on the rocky side of Fall Mountain were for some time jocosely called 'the Governor's calf pasture.'" Almost worthless when selected, portions of the 500 acres have become exceedingly valuable, owing to the superior pine timber found there.

BELLOWS FALLS.

New York, 220; White Mountains, 101; Lake Memphremagog, 171; Montreal, 225; Quebec, 306 miles.

BELLOWS FALLS presents may objects of interest to the tourist. For a considerable distance below the falls, the river is very rapid, and picturesque in appearance, and at no place along its whole course is there so much wild grandeur. Above the village the river curves to the eastward and passes close to the base of Mount Kilburn, which rises precipitously to the hight of 828 feet. It then curves slightly towards the west, and rushes wildly over the rocky bed, down through a narrow gorge, and out into a broader channel below. A large rock divides the stream into two channels, each about 90 feet wide. In low water, the river flows into the western channel, and is contracted to about 16 feet in width. The river in passing over the several rapids makes a descent of 42 feet. The toll and railroad bridges cross the river over the falls, and from the former, a good view of them is had. Below the bridge numberless pot-holes will be observed of various dimensions, worn in the solid rock. West of the station rises a high hill, and beyond it is a valley, only a few feet above the river bank. It is supposed by geologists, that this was once the bed of the Connecticut, and the many terraces in the vicinity strengthens this opinion. It is also claimed, that the region above the falls was once a vast lake, and that its outlet flowed eastward into the Merrimack, from a point further north. Bellows Falls received its name from Col. Bellows, the founder of Walpole, and it was formerly a great fishing place with the Indians, who came here to catch shad and salmon. The latter were so numerous, even after the whites settled in this region, that workmen in making yearly contracts for their labor, stipulated that they should not be obliged to eat salmon oftener than twice a week—a condition, which, at the present time, they would hardly be so particular to require. The first bridge across the Connecticut, was built at this place in 1785, and was 365 feet in length. For eleven years, it was the only bridge across this river.

The Rutland and Burlington Railroad, now operated by the Central Vermont Railroad Company, and the Cheshire Railroad, terminate here. They make connections with Saratoga on the west, and Boston on the east.

One of those ridiculous incidents, which are sufficient to produce a smile at a funeral, occurred on the Cheshire Railroad, early in the winter of 1865. A lady of venerable aspect appeared on the platform at the depot in Bellows Falls, with the inevitable bandbox and bundle. She paced up and down the platform, in a very happy frame of mind, beguiling herself in humming a cradle song, and to all appearances, was at peace with herself and the "rest of mankind." In due season Conductor Stone appeared and shouted "all aboard." The old lady

"I THOUGHT THAT'S THE WAY YOU ALWAYS STOPPED."

not heeding the admonition, he inquired her proposed destination. "Going to Fitchburg, sir," was her reply. "Well, Madam, you had better get into those cars if you want to go to Fitchburg." "What! doesn't this whole consarn go?" alluding to the depot. "Not to-day, madam; you had better get into that car." "Wall, now, mister, is that so? Jist carry this bundle—I never rid a rod on a railroad in my life." The old lady was escorted on board and the train departed. Passing the summit and descending into the Ashuelot Valley, near Keene, the passenger train overtook the freight, out of steam, and "stalled" in the deep snow. It moved up to the freight train, and was about to give it aid, when down came an engine under full headway. A severe snow storm was raging, and so completely obscured the track, that the signal man, who had been sent back, was not seen. It thundered on at a fearful rate down the grade, and in an instant, ran its whole length completely inside of the rear car. Several persons were instantly killed, and others were groaning horribly from injury and fright. The passengers leaped out of doors and windows, and for a while great consternation prevailed. The conductor, as he saw nothing of the old lady, thought it more than probable that she had been killed. He entered the car in search of her, and to his great astonishment, found her sitting quietly alone. Notwithstanding she had made a complete somersault over the seat in front, and her bundle had gone unceremoniously down the aisle, she maintained a wonderfully placid expression upon her countenance, exhibiting neither fear nor astonishment. "Are you hurt?" inquired the conductor. "Hurt, why?" said the old lady. "We have just been run into by an engine, two or three passengers have been killed, and several others severely injured," replied the conductor. La me; I didn't know but that was the *way you always stopped!*"

CHARLESTOWN.

Passing the small station at South Charlestown, you come to Charlestown, eight miles from Bellows Falls. The village, which will be seen east of the railroad, is one of the oldest in western New Hampshire. It was formerly known as Number Four, and, in 1747, a garrison of 30 men, commanded by Capt. Phineas Stevens, was attacked by 400 French and Indians, who, after making a three-days' siege, were obliged to abandon the project and return to Canada. When commanded to surrender by the French General, who boasted of his superior numbers, and of the probable massacre that would take place when the fort was captured, Capt. Stevens very coolly replied: "I can assure you my men are not afraid to die." Sir Charles Knowles, a British naval officer at Boston, when he learned of Capt. Stevens' bravery, presented him an elegant sword, and, from this circumstance, when the township was incorporated, it was named Charlestown.

SPRINGFIELD.

This is the station for Springfield, Vt. The village is on Black River, about six miles west of the railroad. A large manufacturing business is conducted there.

NORTH CHARLESTOWN.

At this station, five miles from Charlestown, a fine view of Ascutney Mountain is had, west of the

Connecticut. The scenery, on the west, in the valley, is exceedingly picturesque.

CLAREMONT.

Twelve miles from Windsor, and fourteen from Bellows Falls, is Claremont Station. The village is two miles east of the railroad. It contains five thousand inhabitants, and there is a large manufacturing interest in the place.

SUGAR RIVER BRIDGE.

Soon after leaving Claremont Station, you come to the bridge over Sugar River. This stream furnishes water power for the manufactories at Claremont. The bridge is 600 feet long and 105 above the river. On the west bank of the Connecticut, from this place, will be seen Ascutneyville, a small village in Wethersfield.

ASCUTNEY MOUNTAIN.

This mountain, which is seen on the west side of the Connecticut, is 3,320 feet high, and is situated in Windsor and Wethersfield. It is an isolated peak, and its bold and rocky summit forms a prominent feature in the landscape for many miles around. Three deep valleys extend down the western slope of the mountain, and from this fact, it is stated, the Indians called it Ascutney, signifying, "Three Brothers." The view from the summit is the most extensive in Eastern Vermont, and very grand. Below is the beautiful Connecticut, winding among the hills and forests, while hundreds of farm houses and villages are scattered seemingly over a vast plain. A road has been constructed from Windsor to the summit, a distance of five miles, and horses and guides can be obtained at Windsor. There is a rude house on the mountain, to protect the tourist in case of storm.

CORNISH.—BIRTH-PLACE OF CHIEF JUSTICE CHASE.

Cornish is situated opposite Windsor. The late Chief Justice Chase was born here. The house in which he was born was torn down a few years since. It stood near the railroad, a mile south of Windsor.

WINDSOR.

From Sugar River Bridge to Windsor the scenery is grand and beautiful. Below, on the west, is the Connecticut, while, still beyond, rises the lofty summit of Ascutney, the grim sentinel of the valley. Crossing the bridge over the Connecticut, just north of the village, you again enter Vermont. Here, nestling among the shade trees upon the hillside, is the ancient and beautiful town of Windsor. The Vermont State Prison is located at this place, on a street west of Main. The constitution of Vermont was formed and adopted in this town, and the building in which the convention was held is still standing on Main street, occupied as a shop. Hon. Wm. M. Evarts and E. W. Stoughton, distinguished members of the New York bar, have summer residences here. Mr. Evarts owns a large farm north of the village, the extensive buildings on which are seen just after leaving the depot, west of the railroad.

West of the depot is seen the United States Court House, built, at great expense, by the United

States Government. And this reminds us of a little story which had its origin in Keene, N. H. Several years since, a certain deputy sheriff officiated as crier of the court. He had a peculiar habit of exclaiming, when some forgotten incident

"BY THE WAY, GOD SAVE THE COMMONWEALTH!"

was recalled to mind, "By the way." As he rose to open the Court, one day, he repeated the usual formula: "Oh yes, all persons having anything to do before the Court of Common Please, will draw near, give their attention, and they shall be heard." At this point, he sat down; but as he did so, he remembered that he had omitted an important part. Instantly rising, he extended the forefinger of his right hand and nervously exclaimed: "By the way, God save the Commonwealth." Even the Court smiled audibly as the crier took his seat.

HARTLAND.

Four miles north of Windsor is Hartland. Before reaching the depot, you cross Lull's Brook, which is seen coursing its winding way down a narrow valley, and from the cars can be seen a beautiful waterfall. This stream received its name from Timothy Lull, of Dummerston, the first settler of the town, who, with his wife and children, came up the Connecticut, in a canoe, in 1763, and landed at the mouth of the brook. Taking out a bottle, and breaking it, in presence of his little family, he gave his own name to the little stream, by which it has since been known. The valley in this vicinity is rich in alluvial deposits, but after passing the depot, the aspect of the country is soon changed, the soil being light and sandy.

NORTH HARTLAND.

This station is four miles from Hartland, and six from White River Junction. Passing North Hartland, you come to the valley of Otta Quechee River. Here the railroad crosses that stream on a bridge 650 feet long, and about 80 feet above the water. As you pass over the bridge, you will notice the beautiful waterfall west of the railroad, where the Quechee makes a perpendicular descent of about fifteen feet. The name of this river is of Indian origin, and was formerly called Ottageeche, taking its name from the manner in which the water tumbles and whirls down the rocks at the falls.

WHITE RIVER JUNCTION.

New York, 260; White Mountains, 61; Lake Memphremagog, 105; Montreal, 185; Quebec, 266 miles.

BEFORE reaching the station, the village of Lebanon, in New Hampshire, on the east bank of the Connecticut, will be seen in full view. The most prominent building is Tilden Female Seminary, a flourishing institution. White River Junction is one of the most important railroad stations on the line. From this point, trains from the North, South, East, and West, meet. The Central Vermont Railroad here passes into the valley of White River, and pursues a more westerly course to Burlington, St. Albans and St. Johns, connecting at the latter place with the Grand Trunk, which extends to Montreal, while the Northern New Hampshire Road, forming here a junction with it, crosses the Connecticut, and connects at Concord, N. H., with other roads leading into Boston. The Connecticut and Passumpsic Rivers Railroad extends from this place in a northerly course, crossing White River at its mouth, just north of the station, to Newport, on Lake Memphremagog, and Sherbrook, on the Grand Trunk, whose passengers make close connections with trains for Quebec. It passes through the rich and fertile valleys of the Connecticut and Passumpsic Rivers. White Mountain tourists proceed on this line to Wells River, forty miles distant, and there take the cars of the White Mountain Railroad to Littleton, Twin Mountain Station, and Fabyan's, the latter within four miles of the Crawford House.

The trains stop at White River Junction for dinner, both going and coming.

NORWICH AND HANOVER.

Five miles from the junction, you come to Norwich and Hanover, the former in Vermont, and the latter in New Hampshire. The villages are about three-fourths of a mile from the station.

DARTMOUTH COLLEGE.

In the beautiful village of Hanover, N. H., a short distance from the depot, on a plain considerably elevated above the Connecticut, is Dartmouth College. This is one of the oldest colleges in New England, only Harvard, Yale and Brown preceding it chronologically. Founded in 1769, it is nearing its centennial. The only college in New Hampshire, it has trained most of the eminent men in the State, and from its high reputation has drawn students from all parts of the country. It has been well said, that it is to the intellectual landscape of the State, what Mt. Washington is to the physical. In every section of the land, and in every walk of life, its sons have attained distinction. Thirteen of them have been Governors, of six different States, thirty-one have been Judges of the Supreme Court, in various States, or of the Federal Courts; four have been members of the Cabinet at Washington, five have occupied diplomatic stations abroad; and one has been Chief Justice of the United States. The contributions of the college to the cause of education, have been especially large. Twenty-two of its alumni have been Presidents of twenty-one different colleges; seventy-eight have been College Professors, twelve of them in various Medical chairs; and thirteen have been Professors of twelve different Theological Seminaries. It has educated more than 800 men for the pulpit. On the roll of its alumni, among other honored names, we note those of Daniel Webster, Rufus Choate, George P. Marsh, and Salmon P. Chase. In addition to the Classical, it has a Scientific and a Medical Department. It has, besides the President, Rev. Asa D. Smith, D.D., L.L. D., twenty Professors. The war drew heavily upon the classes—a large number of the students serving in every capacity, from that of a private, to that of a Major-General. There are four halls for the Classical department, a Scientific building, a Medical college, and an observatory. The latter commands a delightful view down the valley of the Connecticut, the vista ending with Mt. Ascutney. A gymnasium, 47 by 90 feet, has been erected at a cost of $24,000, the gift of Geo. H. Bissell, Esq., of the city of New York, a graduate of the college; and measures are in progress for the erection of an imposing Alumni Hall. The tourist would greatly enjoy a few days in Hanover and vicinity. The rides, in every direction, are pleasant, and during the summer season there is a great influx of agreeable company from the cities.

Among the students there have always been some dependent, mainly, for the means of prosecuting their studies on their own exertions. Such men have usually spent a portion of the winter in school-teaching. In Whittier's beautiful poem—"Snow-Bound," there is a picture of the Dartmouth School-master, which will awaken pleasant memories in many minds:

> "Brisk wielder of the birch and rule,
> The master of the district school,
> Held at the fire, his favored place,
> Its warm glow lit a laughing face,
> Fresh-hued and fair, where scarce appeared
> The uncertain prophecy of beard.
> He played the old and simple games
> Our modern boyhood scarcely names,
> Sang songs, and told us what befalls
> In classic Dartmouth's college halls.
> Born the wild northern hills among,
> From whence his yeoman father wrung
> By patient toil, subsistence scant,
> Not competence, and yet not want,
> He early learned the power to pay
> His cheerful, self-relient way;
> Could doff at ease his scholar's gown
> To peddle wares from town to town;
> Or, through the long vacation reach,
> In lonely lowland districts teach,
> Where all the droll experience found
> At stranger hearths in boarding round;
> The moonlight skater's keen delight
> The sleigh-drive through the frosty night,

The rustic party, with its rough
Accompaniment of blind man's buff,
And whirling plate, and forfits paid,
His winter task a pastime made.
Happy the snow-locked homes, wherein
He tuned his merry violin,
Or played the athlete in the barn,
Or held the good dame's winding yarn,
Or mirth provoking versions told
Of classic legends, rare and old,
Wherein the scenes of Greece and Rome
Had all the commonplace of home,
And little seemed at best the odds
'Twixt Yankee peddlers and old gods;
Where Pindus-born Araxes took,
The guise of any grist-mill brook,
And dread Olympus, at his will,
Became a huckleberry hill.

A careless boy that night he seemed;
But at his desk he held the look
And air of one who wisely schemed.
And hostage from the future took
In trained thought and love of book.
Large-brained, clear-eyed,—of much as he
Shall Freedom's young apostles be,
Who, following in War's bloody trail,
Shall every lingering wrong assail;
All chains from limb and spirit strike,
Uplift the black and white alike;
Scatter before their swift advance
The darkness and the ignorance,
The pride, the lust, the squalid sloth,
Which nurtured Treason's monstrous growth,
Made murder pastime, and the hell
Of prison torture possible.
The cruel lie of caste refute,
Old forms remould, and substitute
For Slavery's lash the Freeman's will,
For blind routine, wise-handed skill;
A school house plant on every hill,

> Stretching in radient nerve lines thence
> The quick wires of intelligence,
> Till North and South together brought,
> Shall own the same electric thought,
> In peace a common flag salute,
> And, side by side, in labor's free
> And unresentful rivalry,
> Harvest the fields wherein they fought."

THE DARTMOUTH STUDENT AND THE CHELSEA CLERK.

Several years since, one of those students at Dartmouth, who, as Whittier says, in the above lines,

> "Could doff at ease his scholar's gown
> To peddle wares from town to town,"

entered the village store at Chelsea, Vt., in search of a customer for some of the books that he was selling. Inquiring of the clerk, one of those over-smart, self-sufficient young men sometimes met with, who resembled an Indian in complexion, if he would like to purchase, the following colloquy took place, in the presence of the usual number of country-store loungers: *Clerk*—"Well, yes, I should like to trade with you if you have a particular work that I am desirous of obtaining." *Student*—"I do not know that I have it, but I presume I can get it for you—what is it?" *Clerk*—"It is Davis' treatise on the Androscoggin River." *Student*—"I am sorry to say, sir, that I haven't it; but I have here a work, which I think is of some importance to you. It is an elaborate treatise on the North American Indians, and I am authorized by the publishers to sell it to *any remnant of the several tribes at half-price!*"

NORWICH UNIVERSITY.

This institution is located about three-fourths of a mile from the Norwich and Hanover depot, and about a mile and a half from Dartmouth College. It was established in 1820, by Capt. Alden Partridge, under the name of the American Literary, Scientific, and Military Academy, and continued in a flourishing condition until Capt. Partridge removed the school to Middletown, Conn. The Middletown school was afterward discontinued, and the principal returned to Norwich. In 1834 a charter was obtained for the Norwich University, and among those who have graduated at this institution, are, Hon. Thomas H. Seymour, of Connecticut; Rev. Theophilus Fisk; Hon. Henry W. Cushman; Hon. Mr. Morse, of Louisiana, formerly member of Congress; Hon. Horatio Seymour, of New York; Hon. William L. Lee, late Chief Justice of the Sandwich Islands; Hon. Caleb Lyons, L.L. D.; Rev. C. H. Frary; Rev. D. S. C. M. Potter; Rev. Josiah Swett, D.D.; Robert Frazer, Esq.; Prof. Alonzo Jackman, L.L. D.; Gen. Robert Millroy; Gen. T. G. Ransom; Gen. Dodge; Col. Clark, of New Hampshire; Col. Jesse A. Gove; Col. F. Farrar; Col. Thomas H. Whipple; Col. Simon Preston; Col. Burton; Col. G. A. Brearex; and Col. T. B. Ransom, who fell at Chepultepec, Mexico, and who succeeded Capt. Partridge as President of Norwich University, after his resignation. Capt. Partridge, who was a native of Norwich, was buried in the town. The main building was burned in 1866, and efforts were then made to rebuild it, but without success. The school has since been removed to Northfield, Vt.

POMPANOOSUC.

Following close upon the bank of the Connecticut, you come to Pompanoosuc station. This was formerly called Ompompanoosuc, an Indian name, given to the little stream that you cross before reaching the station, and signifying a river where onions are found. A few miles north of the station, the first view of the summit of Moose Hillock is had, opposite Newbury, in New Hampshire. Eastward will be seen the rounded form of Bald Mountain.

THETFORD AND LYME.

The village of Thetford is about a mile west of the station. Lyme is on the east side of the river, in New Hampshire.

NORTH THETFORD.

The scenery along the Connecticut continues picturesque and beautiful. From this station is shipped copper ore from Vershire to Portsmouth, and thence to Baltimore by water, where it is smelted.

FAIRLEE AND ORFORD.

Approaching the station, the village of Orford will be seen on the opposite side of the river, in New Hampshire. Here is located a female seminary, seen a short distance east of the river. Passing the station, a ledge of rocks, rising to the hight of two or three hundred feet, will be noticed on the left, resembling a massive wall. Still further north, about five miles from the station, is another, equally as interesting. To the right is a beautiful view of the valley.

BRADFORD.

This is the second most important town between White River Junction and Newport, St. Johnsbury alone exceeding it in point of business. There is considerable manufacturing done here—White's River, which is crossed before reaching the station, furnishing the water power. Three thousand fish kits are manufactured weekly by a single firm, and are sent to Boston. Passengers for Topsham, Corinth, Orange, Washington, and Piermont stop at this station. In this town, in 1812, was manufactured, by James Wilson, the first artificial globe made in the United States.

HAVERHILL—MOOSE HILLOCK.

After leaving Bradford, you come in sight of Haverhill, N. H., situated upon a hill overlooking the valley. Formerly this was the headquarters of the stage lines extending through Northern New Hampshire, and, in those days, was a place of considerable note. As you proceed north from Haverhill, the valley is wide in extent, and the meadows broad and fertile. In New Hampshire, east of Haverhill, you will notice Moose Hillock, rising to the hight of 3,636 feet, the summit of which is the first point seen from this region, to indicate the approach of winter. Sugar Loaf and Black Mountain are nearer to you, further up the river. Prof. Huntington, and others, spent the winter, several years since, on this mountain, making observations.

NEWBURY.

Before arriving at Newbury, you will notice the village on the left, standing on a terrace nearly a hundred feet above the meadows. The railroad passes through a tunnel, made in the narrow terrace, extending eastward from the village. Newbury is one of the oldest towns on the upper Connecticut, and few places present greater attractions for a quiet summer residence. The village, which lies upon high table land, overlooking the broad meadows, contains several stores, two hotels, and the Wesleyan Academy, a Methodist institution. Here are the celebrated Newbury Sulphur Springs, long known to invalids in New England. The scenery in and around Newbury combines the beautiful and the grand. Here you have broad meadows, lofty mountain peaks, and a majestic river, and the view from the adjacent mountains resembles that from Mount Holyoke, in Massachusetts, more than any other point in the Connecticut Valley. Directly in rear of Newbury is Mount Pulaski, an elevation easy of access, and from it can be seen a wide extent of country.

Among the distinguished residents of Newbury in earlier days, were Gen. Jacob Bayley and Col. Thomas Johnson, both of whom took active part in the French and Revolutionary wars. Col. Johnson was in the British service at Crown Point, where, for want of provisions, horse-beef was dealt out to the men. At the opening of the Revolution, he entered the army, and was finally taken prisoner and sent to Canada. He was paroled, and permitted to return home, on condition that he would not again take up arms, and would return when called upon. Gen. Bayley was an important man to the inhabitants of this region, and the British determined upon his capture. June 17, 1782, Capt. Pritchard and a force of British troops, came to Newbury to take him prisoner. Reaching the hights west of the Ox-Bow, they signaled Col. Johnson, and he went to them. He learned the object of the expidition, and on giving them some trifling information, returned home. Gen. Bayley and two sons were in the meadows plowing, near the Ox-Bow. Johnson wrote a message, and directed his wife's brother to leave it in the field, where the General would find it. Dudley Carlton, the bearer of the message, dropped it in the furrow, and on coming to it, Gen. Bayley took it up and read, "The Philistines be upon thee, Samson." That was enough for him. He turned out his team and escaped. That night an attack was made on his house, but he was not there to be captured, as his enemies had expected. There is now a house standing in the Johnson village, south of the Ox-Bow and east of the railroad, that was built in 1775, by Col. Johnson. The frame was raised on the day that news reached Newbury, of the battle of Lexington. Three of the men, who were at the "raising," enlisted, and were at the battle of Bunker Hill. One of the number, Peter Johnson, a brother of the Colonel's was wounded in the arm.

THANKSGIVING POSTPONED FOR WANT OF MOLASSES.

As ludicrous as it may seem at the present time, in the early settlement of the town, Thanksgiving Day was actually postponed two weeks in Newbury, for want of molasses. Communication with the larger towns, was then difficult. Thanksgiving was appointed by the Colonial authorities, having jurisdiction over this reigon, and, as it happened, the proclamation did not reach Newbury until after the appointed day had passed. The minister, on the following Sabbath, read the proclamation, and said that, inasmuch as the day had gone by, he would suggest that the following Thursday, be observed by the people of the town, as a day of Thanksgiving and prayer. A worthy deacon, who enjoyed the good things of life, as well as things spiritual, rose and said, that as there was no molasses in town, and his boys had gone to Number Four (Charlestown, N. H.,) to get some, he would move that Thanksgiving be postponed one week. The "boys" not returning, the day was again postponed, and, finally, the good people of Newbury were obliged to go without their molasses altogether. As it is inferred from this, there was no "sweetning" in the place, a thoughtful housewife wonders what they did for pumpkin pies.

THE GREAT OX-BOW.

The Great Ox-Bow, just north of the village of Newbury, is an object of great interest to tourists. In its southern course, the Connecticut bears off to the east, and thence back to the west, making a circuit of four and a half miles, while across the neck it is only a hundred rods.

WELLS RIVER.

Leaving Newbury, and passing the Great Ox-Bow you soon come to the pleasant village of Wells River, in the town of Newbury, 40 miles from White River Junction. Here White Mountain tourists change cars. This is the junction of the Boston and Montreal, the White Mountains, the Wells River and Montpelier Railroads. It is 20 miles to Littleton, from which tourists, to the Profile House, go 11 miles by stage. The view at this point is magnificent. The Franconia range skirts the eastern horizon. Leaving the station you cross Wells River, a small stream which furnishes power for the mills along its banks.

MC INDOE'S FALLS.

The Connecticut is narrower and more rapid as you approach its source. Several miles below McIndoe's, you pass Dodge's Falls, where the river makes a considerable descent. At McIndoe's the falls are still higher, and furnish excellent water power. After passing the station, you will notice a cove in the river, formed by a huge rock extending from the bank. The river here is only about 75 feet wide, and so rapid, that an iron bar thrown into it would not sink.

BARNET.

Passing McIndoe's, you soon come to Barnet. The village is west of the railroad, mostly upon the hill. This town was granted to two sons of Phineas Stevens, who so gallantly defended the fort at Charlestown, against the French and Indians. It was settled principally by Scotch.

PASSUMPSIC RIVER.

Soon after leaving Barnet, you come to the mouth of the Passumpsic River, which empties into the Connecticut. The Indian name is Bassoomsuc, signifying a stream where there is much medicine. It is so tortuous that it resembles a gigantic cork-screw, liquefied. In a distance of 25 miles, the railroad crosses the river twenty-three times.

THE ISLANDS.—DIGGING FOR GOLD.

In the Connecticut River, just below the mouth of the Passumpsic, there are no less than fifteen islands. The most prominent one is Gold Island, covered with spruce and cedar. Many years ago, some persons, who had been led to believe that the Indians had buried gold there, dug the island over in search of it, but their efforts were not rewarded with a yield of the precious metal. Between this place and Lunenburg, Vt., are the famous fifteen miles falls in the Connecticut.

MC LERAN'S AND PASSUMPSIC.

A short distance above the mouth of the Passumpsic is McLeran's. Before the railroad was built from Wells River to Littletown, this was the starting point for stages to the White Mountains. The falls in the Passumpsic will be noticed on the right. Four miles from here is Passumpsic station.

ST. JOHNSBURY.

Leaving Passumpsic you soon come to St. Johnsbury, the most important station on the line. This is the shire town of Caledonia County, and the Court House will be noticed upon the eminence west of the depot. The village has an unusually neat and thrifty appearance, and the elegant and costly school-houses, which have been erected within the last few years, speak well for the industry and intelligence of the people. There are about 5000 inhabitants in the town.

THE FAIRBANKS SCALES.—GOVERNOR FAIRBANKS.

The life of St. Johnsbury is the Fairbanks Scale Manufactory, where are employed nearly 500 hands. It is situated on Sleeper's River, west of Main Street. With a small beginning this establishment has grown to mammoth proportions, and at the present time, the Fairbanks Scales are used almost throughout the civilized world. Indeed, they have become so general, that it is much easier to tell where they are not used than where they are. They are the invention of Mr. Thaddeus Fairbanks, the only surviving member of the original firm, composed of three brothers, Erastus, Thaddeus and Joseph P. Fairbanks. Like most inventions, this had its origin in almost a trifling circumstance, and has far surpassed even the intention and expectation of the inventor. In 1829, there was an excitement among the farmers, in Vermont and New York, concerning the cultivation of hemp. Erastus and Thaddeus Fairbanks were then engaged in manufacturing plows, stoves, etc., and a company in Lamoille County, applied to them to build a hemp dressing machine. After completing it, they built one for themselves, having determined to carry on the business of hemp dressing, in addition to that which they were already doing. When the farmers began to bring in their hemp, there was at once a want of some arrangement to determine its weight while upon the wagon, so as to save time and labor. The active brain of Thaddeus was called in requisition, and he finally succeeded in perfecting a rude contrivance for weighing the hemp, but containing essentially the principles now used in the scales. At that time transactions by weight were confined to the use of the Even Balance, the Dearborn Beam, and the Roman Steelyards. Erastus saw its importance, and advised his brother to obtain a patent. Application was made, and a patent granted, bearing date of the year 1830. At this time it was not intended to apply the principle to scales only for weighing hemp, hay and other agricultural products; but there being a demand for them in other branches of business, their modifications have been multiplied until they now number 125—from the neat letter balance of a fractional ounce to the ponderous weighlock scale of 500 tons. This was the origin of the Fairbanks Scale, and, although the hemp excitement was of short duration, it produced one of the most important inventions to the business world, that has ever been perfected. A patent was taken out by them in England, and a Liverpool firm engaged in the manufacture of the scales, but subsequent improvements and great accuracy have made those of American manufacture the most popular, even in England and through all Europe. Before the opening of the railroad to St. Johnsbury, all their freight was carried by teams to Portland and Burlington. Ex-Governor Erastus Fairbanks, was a man of more than ordinary ability, although his advantages for an early education were quite limited. He was born at Brimfield, Mass., Oct. 28, 1792, and was a son of a poor farmer. His father being unable to give him an education, he attended only the district school, from which he "graduated" at the age of 17. In May, 1812, he left home and went to St. Johnsbury, to reside with Judge Ephraim Paddock, a maternal uncle, and in whose office it was his intention to study law. His eyes being too weak to admit of his pursuing a course of study, he abandoned the plan, and the two subsequent winters taught the district school, on the plain in St. Johnsbury. In the summer of 1813 he was clerk in a store at Windsor. In 1848, he opened a store at Wheelock, north of St. Johnsbury, in connection with Mr. Fredric Phelps, of St. Johnsbury, who furnished the goods—Mr. Fairbanks' only capital, at this time, being a horse and wagon, which his father had given him, and which he subsequently sold to a hatter for $75, taking his pay in hats. He finally purchased the goods of Mr. Phelps for $800, giving a note for them, to be payed the following winter in ashes. In 1818, he sold his store in Wheelock, and removed to East

St. Johnsbury, where he opened another. In the autumn of that year he went to Barnet, where he remained in the mercantile business until 1824, when he removed to St. Johnsbury, and commenced business with his brothers, who, with their parents, had removed from Brimfield to St. Johnsbury in 1815. They commenced the manufacture of stoves and plows. It was with great difficulty that they found a sale for the plows, as the farmers considered cast iron too brittle a material, to successfully take the place of the rude ones, made of wrought iron and wood. They were obliged to take them to the farmers, where they were left on trial. Finally these plows became quite popular and had a large sale. Governor Fairbanks represented St. Johnsbury in the Legislature in 1835-7-8. In 1844 and 1848, he was chosen Presidential elector on the Clay and Taylor tickets. In 1852 he was elected Governor of Vermont, and in 1864 he died, lamented and loved by all who knew him. The Messrs. Fairbanks have done much to beautify and adorn St. Johnsbury, and their residences are models of neatness and good taste.

Mr. Lincoln and Mr. Blake were exceedingly fond of hunting, and, on one occasion, left town for a day's sport in the woods. They were in the habit of "taking turns" in shooting, and, after frequent consultations with the contents of a certain "little brown jug," they became quite jolly. On the road home, Mr. Blake, not quite in a condition to make correct observations, raised his gun and commenced firing at the horse, which broke away and ran at the first discharge. Neither missed the horse, and the firing was kept up for some moments. Mr. Lincoln, being an exceedingly polite man, had been driving, now turned to his companion and said: "Mr. Blake,

RESULT OF THE FIRST SHOT.

if it is perfectly convenient, you take the lines and let me shoot a while."

ST. JOHNSBURY CENTER.

Three miles north of St. Johnsbury is St. Johnsbury Center. The Passumpsic River lies between the village and the railroad. Here are several manufacturing establishments. Above the depot is a pretty fall in the river.

LYNDONVILLE.

This is a thriving village. Here are located the offices and shops of the Connecticut and Passumpsic Rivers Railroad. A large tract of land was purchased here by the Railroad Company, when Henry Keyes, now deceased, was its President, and the shops and offices were moved here from St. Johnsbury.

WEST BURKE—LAKE WILLOUGHBY.

West Burke, sixteen miles from St. Johnsbury, is the next station. Before reaching the station, you pass Burke Mountain, on your right, 2,000 feet high, and from which there is a magnificent view. Here passengers leave the railroad for Lake Willoughby, six miles distant. Mr. David Trull, proprietor of the West Burke Hotel, near the station, will furnish the tourist conveyance to that place on the arrival of the trains. Willoughby is one of the most remarkable lakes in this country. It lies between two mountains, which rise abruptly from its shores to the hight of nearly 2,000 feet. A carriage road lies close between the east shore of the lake and the mountain, which presents a perpendicular wall 600 feet high. Geologists are of the opinion that, during the drift period, a northern current wore away the calcarious rock, which had become partially decomposed, and left this remarkable gorge. It is a place of great interest to the student of nature. The lake is from half a mile to two miles wide, and is six miles long. The water is so deep, in places, that no bottom has been found. A good

LAKE WILLOUGHBY.

view of Willoughby Mountain, rising from the east shore of the lake, is had before you reach West Burke Station. The summit of the mountain, on the east side, is 2,638 feet high.

SOUTH BARTON—THE SUMMIT—JAY PEAK.

Leaving West Burke, the summit dividing the valleys of the Connecticut and St. Lawrence, is soon reached. You will notice the little rivulet, as you proceed north, running southward, and presently you come to another running north into Crystal Lake, Barton River, Lake Memphremagog, St. Francis River, and thence into the St. Lawrence. Jay Peak, 4,018 feet high, and one of the most lofty summits of the Green Mountain range, will be seen in the north-west. A carriage road has been constructed from the base to the summit, and it can be easily reached from Newport, fourteen miles distant. All the villages near its base, and the mountain peaks for nearly a hundred miles around it, can be seen.

BARTON.

Continuing north, you pass along upon the western shore of Crystal Lake, a small but beautiful sheet of water, and finally come to Barton, at the outlet of the lake, where there is excellent water power. The lake is about a mile wide and two miles long. Barton was named in honor of its first proprietor, Gen. William Barton, who will be remembered as the intrepid Lieut. Col. Barton, of Revolutionary fame. When Lieutenant-Colonel of Rhode Island militia, he, with forty soldiers and a negro, surprised and captured the British Maj.-Gen. Proctor, while in bed at his headquarters, at Newport, R. I. The town was granted to Gen. Barton, Oct. 28, 1781, under the name of Providence, as a reward for this daring exploit. In 1789, its name was changed to Barton.

RUNAWAY POND.

About seven miles south-west of Barton depot, in the town of Glover, is the old bed of Runaway Pond, through which the stage road from Barton to Montpeliar now passes. It was formerly known as Long Pond, and was the source of the Lamoille River, which flows into Lake Champlain. It was about a mile in length, three-fourths of a mile wide, and 150 feet deep, with an outlet at the southern end. About 100 rods north of it was Mud Pond, the outlet of which flowed into Barton River, and thence north into Lake Memphremagog. In dry seasons, Barton River, being insufficient to supply the mills along its banks, with water, it was determined to change the outlet of Long Pond by digging a channel from it to Mud Pond. In June, 1810, the inhabitants of Glover and adjacent towns assembled, in great numbers, for that purpose. It was commenced within a short distance of Long Pond, and completed to Mud Pond. The small barrier at the head of the Pond was then removed, and, instead of following the channel, the water descended into the sand beneath. The stream continued to increase, and finally the whole body of water rushed with great force toward Mud Pond, carrying everything before it. Passing through Mud Pond and into the Barton River, it gathered force as it went. A path thirty or forty rods wide, and from twenty to sixty feet deep was hollowed out by the water. Trees, mills, and even rocks of many tons weight were carried away. So powerful was the current that, after having gone seventeen miles, a rock weighing a hundred tons was moved several rods. It kept on its course until it finally passed into Lake Memphremagog. No lives were lost, but the workmen barely escaped. It seems that beneath the surface, at the head of the pond, was a bed of quick-sand, and, once opened, there was nothing to prevent the water from wearing a channel deep enough to drain the whole pond. A similar occurrence took place in Switzerland in 1818.

BARTON LANDING.

Here are several stores and a saw mill. The village received its name from the fact, that smuggled goods were brought up the river from Canada and landed here. A daily stage runs from this place to Irasburg, three and a half miles westward, and which is one of the prettiest villages in Northern Vermont.

COVENTRY.

Leaving Barton Landing, you soon reach Coventry Station. The village lies several miles west of the railroad. Continuing northward, you come to a bay connected with Lake Memphremagog. Passing along its eastern bank, you cross it on a pile bridge, and, in a few minutes, are landed near the

Memphremagog House, at Newport, upon the southern end of Lake Memphremagog. For several years this was the terminus of the Connecticut and Passumpsic Rivers Railroad. In May, 1867, the road having been extended, was opened to Derby, at the Canada line, five miles further north, and subsequently, another road was built from Derby to Lennoxville, on the Grand Trunk, where connections are made with Montreal and Quebec.

LAKE MEMPHREMAGOG.

New York, 364; White Mountains, 112; Boston, 234; Montreal, 130; Quebec, 161 miles.

HERE we are, at last, dusty and weary, at Newport, that haven of rest. Not Newport, down by the sea, but Newport, Vt., on the shore of Lake Memphremagog, close to the Canada line, where, years gone by smuggling was counted among the virtues (it doesn't pay as well now), is a thriving, pleasant country village, destined to be a place of considerable importance in the future. The scenery around it is grand and inspiring, and the breezes from the lake are cool and refreshing. South of the village, rising to the hight of two or three hundred feet, is Prospect Hill, overlooking the lake and the country for miles around. From it is seen Owl's Head, Mt. Elephantis, Mt. Orford, Jay Peak, and Willoughby Mountain. The view of the lake, with its islands and bays, is remarkably fine, especially at sunset, when all nature is tinged with a golden hue.

The Memphremagog House has long been a favorite with pleasure seekers. It is situated upon the shore of the lake, and near the depot. The landlord, W. F. Bowman, is well known to tourists. The growth and prosperity of this village is comparatively of recent date. The opening of the rail-

THE MEMPHREMAGOG HOUSE.

road brought pleasure seekers to the lake, and gave the place increased business and new life. Its growth has been rapid, and, in many respects, reminds one of a smart western town, just budding into existence. The people are social and hospitable, gladly welcoming all who come to spend the summer here. They are industrious and thriving; but there is old Mr. Brown, who lives several miles out of the village—he has one very bad habit. He never comes to town without getting drunk. The townspeople, who know his failings, are very kind

OLD MR. BROWN FINDS A CART.

to him. When he has "taken in" more than he can carry, they "lay him out" in his cart, and start his cattle homeward. One day a wag happened to pass Brown just out of Newport, when he was in this sad condition. His faithful team had stopped under a shade tree, evidently reflecting upon Brown's miserable habit. The aforesaid wag quietly disconnected the cattle from the cart and started them toward home. Brown was too drunk to know what had happened; but, several hours afterward, he awoke from his drunken stupor, and, after gazing wildly about, exclaimed: "Well, some one has lost a yoke of cattle, or I've found a cart!"

THE LAKE.

In the great basin that lies between the White and Green Mountains, and on the borders of Vermont and Canada, is Lake Memphremagog, one of the loveliest inland lakes within the limits of New England. Its name is of Indian origin, and signifies Beautiful Water. Though differing in many particulars, in general appearance it more resembles the far-famed Lake George than any other body of water which has come under our observation, and is so regarded by old travelers, who are familiar with both. There are no marshes along its borders, and its shores are rock-bound, while the water is cold and clear as crystal. Here and there are beautiful islands, covered with spruce and other forest trees, adding variety to the scene. On the west shore are high mountains, overlooking the lake and the country around it, while on the east is a long range of hills, sloping down, in places, to the water's edge. The scenery, which is so varied, is quite unlike any found elsewhere in New England, and there is a charm about it that is fascinating to all lovers of the picturesque and beautiful in nature. It matters not whether one is silently studying the myriad forms of beauty spread out before him in so great profusion, or is gazing upon the distant mountain peaks which seem to touch the blue sky above, or is watching the golden shadows flitting across the placid lake, there is something so suggestive, and so beautiful, that the eye never wearies, and the mind is refreshed with this communion with nature. As the steamer plows the lake close up to the lofty mountain, going within its very shadows, and the eye takes in the scenery, so unlike anything that it is accustomed to, the traveler catches the same spirit of inspiration which must have animated those dusky sons of the forest, and lead them to exclaim, when they first looked down from the wood-crowned hights above, upon the long and narrow lake, stretching away to the north, " Memphremagog ! "—Beautiful Water !

There is something, too, in this northern air, that exhilarates and increases one's love of nature. The heavy, murky atmosphere, so oppressive in midsummer, in the over-heated cities, is unknown here on the banks of Memphremagog. The currents of air flowing over and cooled on the high mountain elevations, or come up the lake, seem to give one new life, infusing greater animation. The sunsets, too, are peculiarly beautiful. The blue sky seems almost transparent, while the golden tinge, shed over land and water, gives the face of nature a charm and a coloring that sets the painter's art at defiance. It touches and quickens the inner nature of man, and he longs for a closer intimacy with that Spirit which seems to pervade everything.

The lake is from one to two miles wide on an average, and is thirty miles long, reaching from the village of Newport, in Vermont, on the south, to Magog, a Canadian hamlet, on the north. Full two-thirds of the lake is in Canada, and the boundary

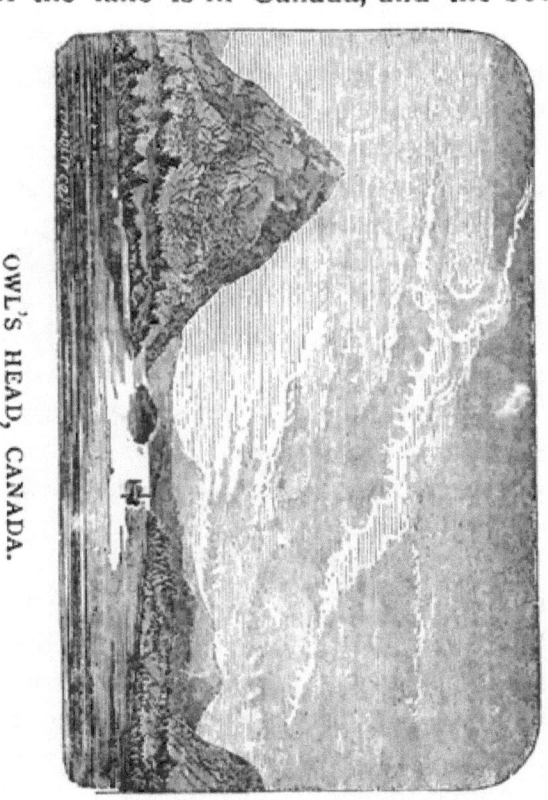

OWL'S HEAD, CANADA.

line is easily distinguished—south of it there being more thrift and enterprise than is seen just north, over the line in Canada. The water in most places is very deep and cold, and is just the place for the lake trout which are caught each year in great abundance. On the east shore of the lake are the summer cottages of some of the wealthiest people of Montreal, who always spend the warm season here.

DOWN THE LAKE.

Refreshed with a night's sleep in this cool and bracing mountain region, the tourist will prepare for a trip on the steamer Lady of the Lake. To your right after leaving Newport, is Indian Point, extending into the lake, long since the abode of the red man. Directly ahead is Bear Mountain, and beyond, further up the lake, is Owl's Head, twelve miles from the Memphremagog House. It towers far above its neighbors, and its peculiarly rounded summit, riven seemingly into immense fisures, will attract your attention. You pass Adams' Bay, on the west, and soon afterward Potten Bay, on the same side of the lake, named after the township in which it is situated.

THE TWIN SISTERS.

Gliding smoothly over the water, past Indian Point, you come in sight of the "Twin Sisters"— two beautiful islands covered with evergreens, and standing near the other shore. Looking between these islands, as the steamer comes abreast of them, you will notice the village of Stanstead, in Canada, ten miles distant.

PROVINCE ISLAND.

Straight ahead is Province Island, containing about 100 acres, most of which was formerly cultivated by a Frenchman, who, with his family, lived here in seclusion. Here Mr. Carlos Pierce, a Boston merchant, now deceased, raised blooded stock.

THE CANADA LINE.

The steamer is making good headway, and you begin to feel the exhilarating influence of the pure air, and the grand mountain and lake scenery. You are now approaching the Canada line, and presently will pass into British waters. In Vermont the farms and farm houses indicate thrift and enterprise, but beyond, in Canada, the country is wild and poorly cultivated. Near the lake shore you will notice a clearing extending westward up the mountain. An iron post marks the dividing line, between the United States and Canada. Eastward, extending across the southern end of Province Island, on the crest of the hill, you will observe a gap in the woods which shows the course of the line on that side of the lake. The steamer's bell is tolled and soon you will pass from the United States to the dominions of Queen Victoria.

TEA TABLE ISLAND.

East of Province Island, and close in shore, is Tea Table Island. It is a charming little spot, covered with cedar, and is just the place for a rural picnic.

CEDARVILLE.

Beyond, on the eastern shore, is Cedarville, in the town of Stanstead. A cedar grove comes down to the lake, and the place has a quiet, rural aspect. The bay extends north of the landing, and terminates in a sharp point.

FITCH'S BAY.

Steaming along you are soon off Fitch's Bay, which extends north-east about seven miles inland.

WHETSTONE ISLAND.

Near the entrance to Fitch's Bay is Whetstone Island, which is remarkable for a quarry of Novalculite, or Magog oil stone, as it has been called. This quarry of Novalculite, which made capital whetstones, was worked some years ago by a company from Burke, but the British government finally put a stop to it.

MAGOON'S POINT.

On the east side of the lake you soon pass Magoon's Point, the grassy slope of which, reaches down to the water. Excellent lime is burnt here, said to be the best in the country. An unexplored cavern exists in this locality, and it has been believed that a large amount of treasure, stolen from a Roman Catholic Cathedral, was secreted there. Indeed, there are persons, who claim to have seen two massive gold candlesticks which were found buried in the road near the cave.

ROUND ISLAND.

As the steamer nears the base of Owl's Head, you pass Round Island on your right. It is only half a mile from the old Mountain House landing, and is frequently visited by tourists. It is covered with cedar, and its rounded form, and rock bound shore give it an interesting appearance. Heading in shore, the steamer glides swiftly up to the wharf, which is situated at the base of Owl's Head, in a sheltered nook, completely shut out from the outside world, except by lake communication. This is twelve miles from Newport, although you can hardly believe it, the time has passed so pleasantly. Tourists ascending Owl's Head leave the steamer at this place. The lake and the Islands in this vicinity,

present a picturesque appearance, and you never tire in be holding the view.

MINNOW ISLAND.

East of the Mountain House, and nearer the eastern shore, is Minnow Island, named from its diminutive size. It is a favorite fishing place, and some of the famous lake trout are caught here.

SKINNER'S CAVE.

East of the Mountain House will be noticed Skinner's Island. On the north-western side, near the end, and close to the water, is Skinner's Cave. It is an interesting locality, and is frequently visited. It is about ten feet wide at the entrance, twelve to fourteen feet high, and extends into the rock a distance of thirty feet, narrowing from the entrance until the two walls meet. There is a legend connected with it, which the late John Ross Dix has

told in verse, but before giving you his story, we will state that it concerns one Uriah Skinner, the bold smuggler of Magog. In the war of 1812, smuggling was extensively carried on between persons residing in Canada and Vermont, and Uriah was the most successful of them all. He, however, was caught at last, as will be seen:

WHAT BECAME OF THE BOLD SMUGGLAR OF MAGOG.

" Fancy a fellow, brawny and brown,
With very black hair that hangs shaggily down,
With whiskers remarkably bushy and black,
With fists which might give a most terrible thwack;

With very fierce eyes under dark heavy brows,
That flashed like a cat's when it springs on a mouse,
Or like coals in a cavern that gleam fiery red,
With a great Roman nose, so uncommonly red,
That whenever he washed it ('twas seldom) I wis,
The water would certainly bubble and hiss!

With a mouth, firm, compressed, and much prone to a sneer,
With a purple scar stretching from chin unto ear;
With a huge dagger stuck in the belt round his waist,
And five or six pistols beside it placed;
With a heavy cutlass not long nor pliant,
Such as little "Jack" used when he slaughtered the "Giant,"

With great heavy boots—and as heavy a purse,
With a tongue that scarce wagged but it uttered a curse!
Fierce as a tiger—as cruel as Nero—
Fancy all these, and you'll picture my hero;
Whose name, for fame has preserved the same,
Was Uriah Skinner, who'd always on hand
Plenty of articles contraband.

Of all the smugglers who plied on the lake,
Uriah Skinner was hardest to take;
The officers hunted him often, and yet
Uriah Skinner they never could get!
For if his boat they e'er chanced to have sight of,
He vanished, as 'twere, and was speedily right off,
Like the Flying Dutchman, he seemed to melt
Into mist; so that some who pursued him, felt
Inclined to believe he had something to do
With a certain dark gentleman—you know who!

The pitcher may often go to the well
Yet at last be broken: so it befell
In the case of Uriah—for that bold chap
Was caught at last like a rat in a trap!

*   *   *   *

Night on the lake, so clear and calm,
The night breeze sings in the pines its psalm;
Stars shine bright in the dark blue sky,
And the cresent moon sails in her glory on high:
Above and below, it is all serene,
Who, as he gazed on the peaceful scene
At that moment, would fancy that nine or ten
Very keen sighted, and well armed men,
Motionless, and still as the dead,
Were ambushed under the great Owl's Head?
And their ears were open as well as their eyes,
Listening and looking alike for the prize;
There they watched to catch the first glimpse or note
Of Skinner, expected that night in his boat,

"Look—don't you see!
That, Skinner must be!"
Oh, Skinner! bold smuggler! there's peril for thee!
For down to the shore with leap and bound,
The officers rush—as goes a blood-hound
On a fugitive's track when the scent is found!
The boat is manned, and they're off the next minute,
They see Skinner's boat, and Uriah S. in it;
Now the chase grows eager and hot,
And Skinner thinks so too, I wot,
For, his boat speeds over the waters blue,
Swiftly as flieth an Indian's canoe,
And he has an Indian's craftiness too;
Now they near him—now they are on
His heels as it were—and now—HE IS GONE!

But where?
How they stare
And rave and swear!
And how—here, there, and everywhere,
The island they search—for they think, like the deer
Who leaves the forest and takes to the floods,
The smuggler has quitted the lake for the woods!
But all they find is the empty boat,
Which one of the officers pushes afloat.
The fruitless search they at length give o'er
And Uriah Skinner was never seen more!
'Tis said that one of the officers swore,
A strong brimstone oder pervaded the shore!
And another averred that he saw Skinner go
In the clutch of old Nick, to the regions below.

Nearly six years had passed away,
When a fisherman out in a storm one day,
Was very near making an awful plunge
To become a meal for the pickerel or longe;
But through the mist gazing eager-eyed,
In the side of an island, a cave he spied,
And in less than a minute, was safe inside.

Very soon passed the storm, and then,
Ere he prepared to go fishing again,

He looked above, beneath, and around,
And what do you think the fisherman found?
Neither a golden nor a silver prize,
But a skull with sockets where once were eyes;
Also some bones of arms and thighs,
And a vertebral column of giant size:
How they got there he couldn't devise,
For he'd only been used to common-place graves,
And knew nought of "organic remains" in caves;

On matters like these, his wits were dull,
So he dropped the subject as well as the skull.

"'Tis needless to say
In this latter day,
'Twas the smuggler's bones in the cave, that lay:
All I've to add is—the bones in a grave
Were placed, and the cavern was called 'SKINNER'S CAVE.'"

LONG ISLAND.—BALANCE ROCK.

North of Skinner's Cave is Long Island. It is about a mile and a half long, and half a mile wide.

It has a bold and rocky shore, and near its northern end, on the western side, are some perpendicular rocks named the Palisades. On the southern shore of the island is the famous Balance Rock, so fre-

BALANCE ROCK.

quently visited by tourists. It is a huge granite rock of many tons weight, resting upon another close to the water's edge and poised upon a single point, as seen in the illustration. How it got into its present position is a matter of speculation.

MOLSON'S ISLAND.

Further north is Molson's Island, on the eastern side of the lake. It is owned by Mr. Molson, a Montreal broker, whose summer residence will be noticed eastward upon the hillside, from which there is a picturesque view.

THE SCENERY.—CANADIAN RESIDENCES.

At this point there is some of the best scenery on the lake. From the west shore, Owl's Head rises abruptly to a greater hight and its cone-like shape will attract your attention. Further north is Mount Elephantis, and in the distance, between the two mountains is Jay Peak. The eastern shore which rises to the hight of several hundred feet above the lake, is adorned with the summer residences of the wealthy business men of Montreal.

MOUNT ELEPHANTIS.

You are now passing Mt. Elephantis or Sugar Loaf, as it is sometimes called. The upper point bears resemblance to an elephant's head and back. As you proceed north, you will observe that this mountain is in the shape of a horse shoe. Within the curve is some excellent farming lands, situated upon an elevated plain above the lake. Capt. Fogg gave this locality the name of "Sebastopal," from its impregnable position.

CONCERT POND.

West of the most elevated point of Mt. Elephantis, lying between that and Ridge Mountain, is Concert Pond. It it several hundred feet above Lake Memphremagog, and abounds in brook trout. It is a favorite fishing place for tourists. The Pond is two miles long and half a mile wide, and the view of it from Mt. Elephantis is exceedingly beautiful.

GEORGEVILLE.

Upon the eastern shore of the lake, about twenty miles from Newport, and seven and a half from the Mountain House, is Georgeville. It contains two

MOUNT ELEPHANTIS.

hotels and several stores, and is the most important place along the lake.

KNOWLTON'S LANDING.

At Georgeville the mail is taken on board and the steamer heads towards Knowlton's Landing, on the west side of the lake. This is the crossing place for the inhabitants in the eastern townships when going to Montreal. For nearly thirty years Capt. Fogg carried the mail across the lake at this place, commencing first with a canoe. The lake is three miles wide, and will average 300 feet in depth, from one shore to the other. Stages run regularly from Knowlton's to Waterloo, 20 miles distant, where they connect with the Stanstead, Shefford and Chambly Railroad, for St. John's and Montreal. Sergeant's Bay extends some five miles inland, northeast from Knowlton's.

GIBRALTAR POINT.

Leaving Knowlton's you pass Gibralter Point on your left. The rocks rise perpendicular from the lake, presenting a magnificent appearance. On the summit, near the southern point, is the boundary corner of four towns—Potten, Bolton, Stanstead and Magog.

LORD'S ISLAND.

Turning Gibralter Point, and coming into the lake again, you get an extensive view. In the distance you will notice Lord's Island, the last one of any importance before reaching Magog.

MOUNT ORFORD.

For some time, in looking north your eye has rested upon an elevation, peering above the distant hills. As you approach the northern end of the lake, its elevated summit is more distinctly seen. This is Mt. Orford, 3,300 feet high, and is the most extensive mountain in Lower Canada. It is five miles from Magog, and a carriage road has been constructed to its summit.

MAGOG.

The steamer's whistle is blown, and you will notice

that she is heading in shore. Ahead is the village of Magog, at the outlet of the lake. The village is somewhat antidiluvian in appearance and you wonder if some of the early settlers did not come over in the ark. Here the water in the outlet makes a

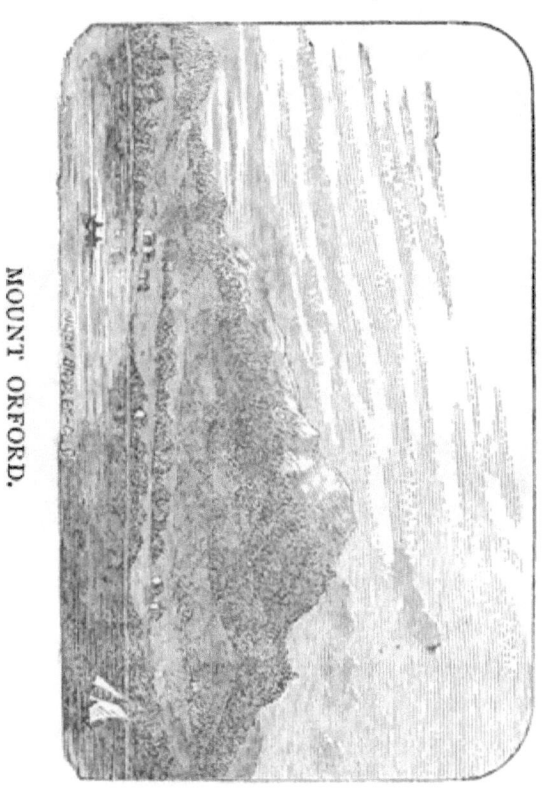

MOUNT ORFORD.

great descent, furnishing excellent power for the many saw mills. Beyond the town, towards the base of Mt. Orford is a wide belt of forest, and for many miles around there is an unlimited supply of the best of timber, principally spruce.

THE RETURN TRIP.

Having spent a short time at Magog, the steamer's whistle is blown, and you go on board to make the return trip. The view up the lake, towards the south, is exceedingly beautiful. In the dim distance lying between Owl's Head and Mt. Elephantis, is Jay Peak, and the Green Mountain range. The sail back is agreeable. Before you reach Newport, you

OWL'S HEAD FROM THE NORTH.

will notice the notch in Willoughby Mountain, 30 miles south of Newport. In this notch lies Lake Willoughby.

THE ASCENT OF OWL'S HEAD.

Leave the steamer at the Mountain House landing to ascend Owl's Head, where a foot path leads to the summit. For a little way the course is tolerably level, but after about ten minutes walking, the ascent commences in earnest. On either side the path is bordered by woods, where wild birds sing and squirrels gambol undisturbed. You may loiter and pick berries and wild flowers, which are very abundant. A maple grove is next passed, and then you arrive at a circular sort of basin named Fern Hollow. Still ascending, you reach Fern Rock, where a botanist might long luxuriate. The way now becomes pretty steep, but if you halt occasionally to recover breath, you may use your eyes as well as rest your lungs, for there are plenty of objects worthy attention. For here is Birch Rock. On the steep hill-side above you are two large, oblong granite rocks—their ends being placed so close together that there does not appear room to place a finger's point between them. Yet in that fisure is sufficient earth to nourish a fine birch tree, which seems to rise from, and grow out of the lower stone. Onward and upward we go, until we are brought to a stand at the Toll-Gate, where it is by no means an unusual thing to find a toll-keeper also. This Toll-Gate is formed by two large rocks, from whose upper surface trees spring upwards, and between which there is just room for one very stout, or two slim persons to walk abrest. Hoops have no chance here, unless the circles are changed to ovals, or elipses. Occasionally a lady has been compelled to retire to a leafy bower, hard by, called Crinoline Chamber, and divest herself of all "hinderances," for a Camel may as well attempt to go through the eye of a needle, as a fashionably dressed lady to get through the Toll-Gate. This perilous "pass" having been accomplished, the next object of attraction is Chair Rock, from whose summit the first view of the lake during the ascent, is obtained. Passing along you come to Breakneck Stairs. Next come Winding Staircase, and then Refreshment Hollow, where your little tin can will be found useful in conveying water from the spring to your lips. Somewhat refreshed, you press forward and soon stand on the summit of Owl's Head—nearly 3,000 feet above the waters of Memphremagog. The prospect is magnificient beyond description. Looking south you see Clyde, Barton and Black Rivers, Newport, all the islands on the lake, and the lake itself from end to end. To the north, Durham's Point, Dewey's Point, Knowlton Bay, the Outlet, Orford Mountain, and countless other objects. To the east, Seymour Lake, Stanstead Plain, Rock Island, Salem Pond, Charleston Pond, Derby Center, Derby Line, Willoughby Lake, White Mountains, Little Magog, Massawippi Lake, Georgeville, &c. To the west, the continuation of the Green Mountain Range. To the north-west, the Sugar Loaf and Ridge Mountain, Broome Lake and North and South Troy. In a clear day Montreal can be distinctly seen in the north-west. The summit itself, as might be expected from its appearance from below, is all split up or riven into gorges and ravines, from which four distinct peaks ascend. In one of these ravines is the Freemason's Lodge, so named from the fact that the Golden Rule Lodge of

Stanstead, hold a lodge there once a year, on the 24th of June. It is a spot well calculated for exercising the mysteries of the craft. On a triangular rock are painted the compass and square, and below that masonic emblem, other inscriptions.

MT. WILLOUGHBY FROM LAKE MEMPHREMAGOG.

After spending a few hours on the summit of Owl's Head, the tourist will descend to the landing and return to Newport, greatly invigorated and pleased with the trip. Before reaching Newport, you will see, on the southern horizon, the summit of Mt. Willoughby, as shown in the accompanying illustration, which is one of the most interesting places to geologists in New England.

RAILROAD CONNECTIONS.

The opening of the Southern Railroad, from

OWL'S HEAD FROM THE RAILROAD ABOVE NEWPORT.

Newport to West Farnham, gives another and shorter route from Lake Memphremagog to Montreal. At West Farnham, connection is made with the road from Waterloo to St. Johns, and at the latter place, with the Grand Trunk, which extends to Montreal. In going to Quebec, the tourist will proceed north to Sherbrook, where connections are made with the cars by the Grand Trunk Railway, forty miles from Newport. At Richmond, 25 miles from Sherbrook, another change is made, this being the junction with the Grand Trunk and its branch to Quebec. The distance from Richmond to Quebec is 96 miles. The ride to Richmond is quite agreeable. Soon after leaving Newport, you will notice, on the left, Owl's Head. This is the finest view of the lake and the mountain that can be had from any point. Passing Stanstead Junction, Libby's Mills, Smith's Mills, and Ayer's Flats, you will soon come upon the eastern shore of Massawippi Lake, along which the road extends for several miles. A junction with the Grand Trunk is made at Lennoxville, but the train runs to Sherbrook, three miles further, before there is a change of cars. From Sherbrook, to Richmond, the railroad runs along the bank of St. Francis River. From Richmond to Point Levi, opposite Quebec, the country is without interest. The villages are small, and the fields uninteresting, being generally poorly cultivated.

THE WHITE MOUNTAINS.

A PRELIMINARY VIEW.

On the northern boundary of New Hampshire are the most elevated mountain summits of New England, the rocky boldness and grandeur of which justly entitle that region to the appellation of "the Switzerland of America." The lofty peaks, the deep and narrow passes, the sublime scenery, touches the poetic nature of man, and he wonders at the mighty power that has shaped such vastness and beauty. The fame of the White Mountains is almost world-wide, although hardly a half century has passed since they were looked upon only by neighboring primitive settlers, or the more daring lover of the sublime in nature. A period of about thirty years will cover the time, since the Mountains were first visited by any considerable number. Small the number at first, the tide of sight-seekers has gradually increased, until now not less than ten thousand people annually visit all or some portions of the various mountains.

Darby Field of Pascataquack, accompanied by two Indians, ascended the highest peak of the White Mountains, in 1642, but the first mention of the mountains in print did not occur until 1672. The

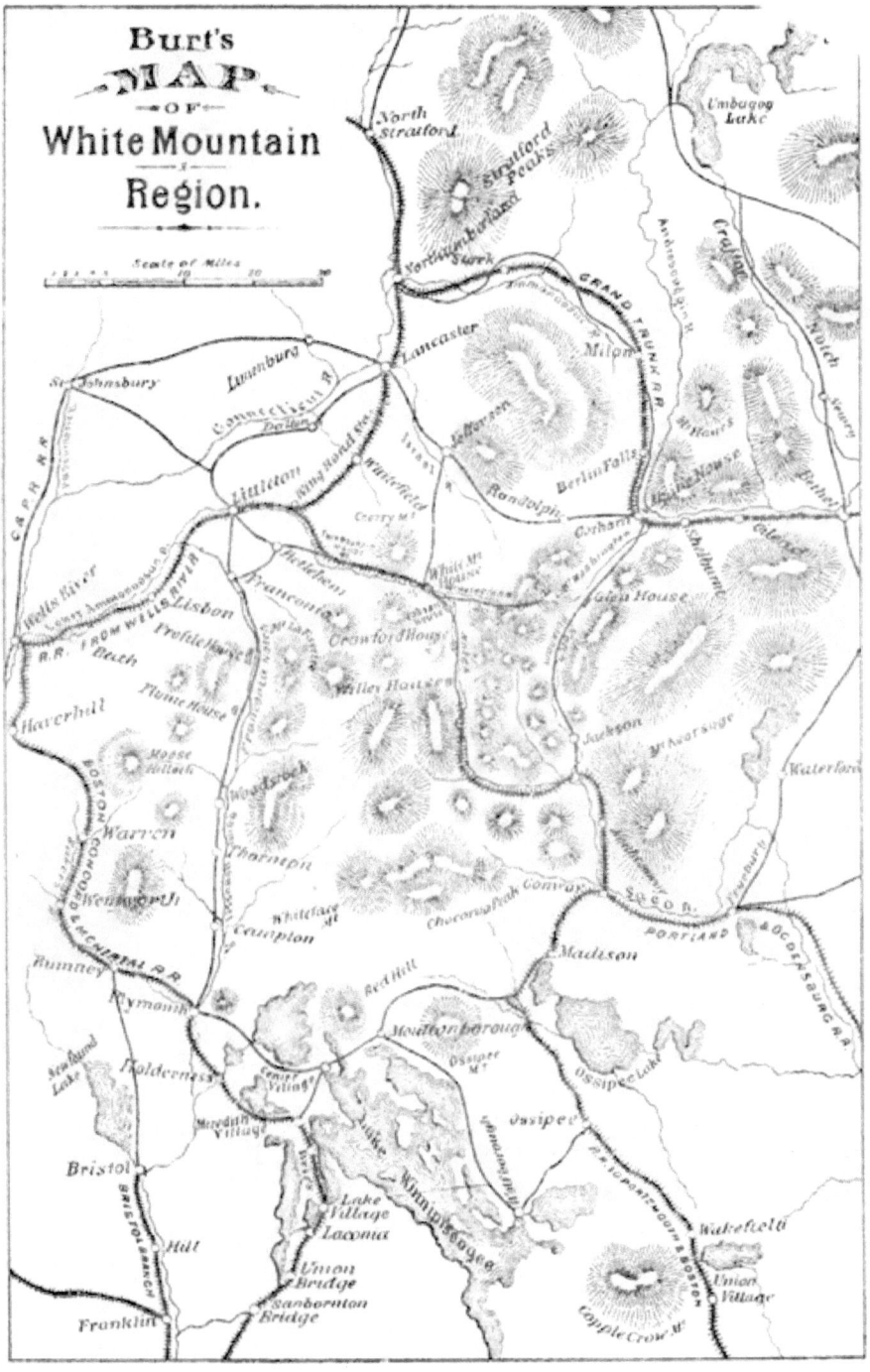

first rude public house, for occasional visitors, was erected upon the Giant's Grave, in 1803, by Eleazer Rosebrook, five miles west of the present Crawford House. In 1819, Abel Crawford and his son Ethan Allen Crawford were the first to clear a path through the woods, to the rocky ridge and in 1840 Abel Crawford, at the age of 75, rode the first horse that climbed the cone of Mt. Washington. The first house on that mountain was built by his son Ethan.

No conception of the grandeur of the view from the summit of Mt. Washington, can be formed without a visit to the mountain itself. The most faithful description, when placed upon paper, is spiritless in comparison with the mighty scene spread before you, from an altitude of more than six thousand feet! While the tide of travel to this wonderful land is increasing year by year, there are thousands who have no realizing sense of the pleasure that they are depriving themselves of, by remaining at home —toiling, perhaps, day after day, in the never ceasing round of business, that a little more may be hoarded for a coming generation to squander. Oh! you man of toil! what will it profit you to wear your very life out in acquiring mere wealth, while the finer instincts of your nature are blotted out, or allowed to run to waste? The White Hills should be cherished by us all, as the Mecca of America, to which it should be a religious duty, to make at least one pilgrimage in our life time!

The opening of new railroads, and the extension of old lines have made the tour of the White Mountains less wearisome. The routes mostly traveled are: Through the Connecticut Valley to White River Junction, Wells River and Littleton; up the Hudson to Lake George and Burlington, and thence to Montreal, Lake Memphremagog, Wells River and Littleton; or direct from Burlington to Montpelier and Wells River; from Boston to Concord, Plymouth, Wells River, and Littleton; or from Boston to Portsmouth and Conway, entering the White Mountain Notch from the east. Each route has some peculiar features of interest. If you have chosen the Connecticut Valley route or that up the Hudson, you change cars at Wells River, and follow the Ammonoosuc to Littleton, a distance of twenty miles. At Littleton you leave the cars for the Profile House, going there by stage. If your destination is the Twin Mountain House, Fabyan's, or the Crawford House, you continue by rail to the Fabyan House. This is at the junction of the Mt. Washington turnpike leading from the Ammonoosuc to the railway, which extends to the summit of Mt. Washington, and is within four and a half miles from the Crawford House.

LITTLETON TO THE PROFILE HOUSE.

The six horse coaches will be in readiness on the arrival of the train at Littleton, to convey the tourist to the Profile House, 11 miles distant. On leaving the village a southerly route is pursued, and shortly you commence to ascend high table land. Within half an hour, and after the ascent is made, you behold on your left the lofty White Mountain range, Mt. Washington standing sentinel over all the rest. Ahead of you is Mt. Lafayette, its deep furrowed sides in full view. Descending slowly you enter the village of Franconia. This, in winter, is one of the coldest places in the mountains, and the thermometer sometimes registers as low as 34 degrees below zero. The south branch of the Ammonoosuc, which rises in the Franconia Mountains, passes through the village. As you leave the valley of the Ammonoosuc and commence the mountain ascent the sun is nearing the western horizon. The golden shadows upon the dark forest trees, which skirt the mountain side, are singularly beautiful. Such a sunset, as is sometimes witnessed here, is rarely seen elsewhere. The long lines of light and shade give that brilliant coloring of purple and gold, which is seen in perfection only in a northern clime.

Soon after leaving Franconia a "slide," a long white line, will be noticed on the side of Mt. Lafayette extending downward. This is just to the right of the Profile House, and seems only a short distance to it; but an hour will be consumed before the hotel is reached. Slowly the coach ascends to the Notch, passing Bald Mountain on your left. As you reach the summit, and commence to descend into the Notch, the base of Mt. Lafayette and its great wall of green impresses you with its vastness and grandeur. In a few minutes you reach the border of Echo Lake, a clear and beautiful sheet a half mile north of the Profile House. A few minutes later the coach is stopped in front of the hotel itself, as the evening twilight begins to deepen.

THE PROFILE HOUSE.

A welcome sight indeed, is the Profile House to the weary traveler, as it greets his vision at the twilight hour. Fatigued by an all-day's ride, he leaves the coach and enters this magnificent hotel, surprised at its extent and the strange wildness of the scene around it. Having satisfied the wants of an appetite that had been sharpened by the ride, he strolls down the carriage road, which is overshadowed by the dark walls above. All nature seems hushed in repose, and naught but the sighing of the wind in the tree tops far above disturbs his meditation. How vast and how mighty seem the everlasting mountains, whose summits are lost to him in the darkness of night! Retracing his steps, he enters the hotel and joins, perhaps, in the merrymaking in the parlor, where a gay and bewitching scene presents itself. Merry voices mingle with sweet music, and joy seems unconfined. The Profile house stands upon the highest ground in the Notch, and is nearly 2,000 feet above the sea. It is completely shut in by the mountains which rise almost from its doors to a great hight, Cannon Mountain, on the west, and Eagle Cliff on the east. Such wildness and grandeur the tourist has seldom seen, and he never tires in gazing upon the varied forms of beauty which, on every hand, meet his view. The hotel, which is a model of neatness and comfort, is kept by Messrs. Tyler & Greenleaf, long known to mountain tourists. It has several times been enlarged to meet the growing popularity of the place, until it will now accommodate 500 guests. The parlor is eighty-four by fifty feet, and 460 yards of carpeting are required to cover its floor. A band of music is always in attendance for the pleasure of guests, and dancing forms one of the attractions of the place during the evening hours. Here is a telegraph office, and the mails are received daily, so that guests, though away from the larger places, are not altogether outside of the comforts and luxuries of home. There are several objects of interest near the hotel that can be reached on foot. First of all, and the great lion of the Notch, is

THE OLD MAN OF THE MOUNTAIN.

There is no single object of so much general interest around the whole mountains, and thousands have looked upon the Titanic features of The Old Man in wonder and astonishment. If the tourist came by the evening coach, he should certainly rise the next morning at an early hour and walk down the carriage road toward the south, a hundred rods from the hotel. Just as he reaches the path leading to the boat house on Profile Lake, he should look upward, to the right, and there will greet his vision the unmistakable outlines of the human profile, projecting from the rugged side of Mt. Cannon, at least 1,000 feet above him. So perfect and so wonderful is the resemblance, he feels a thrill of half surprise and half fear creep over him. He starts back and exclaims, can it be possible that the great forces of nature, by mere chance, have carved such an exact image of the human features upon this great rocky mountain side? Thousands have been here to look upon this, Nature's greatest curiosity, and its fame is told in many a song and legend. The incredulous, however, before looking upon the "Great Stone Face," fancy it must require

THE OLD MAN OF THE MOUNTAIN.

a wide stretch of imagination to witness that which is claimed, but a single glance sweeps away all unbelief. The profile is made up of three separate masses of rock, some distance apart, and the whole length, from forehead to chin is eighty feet. One piece forms the forehead, another the upper lip, and the third the chin. Passing farther down the road, until coming in front, the profile is entirely lost to view. The most favorable time for seeing it is either before the sun shines upon it, or late in the afternoon, after it has passed behind Mt. Cannon.

PROFILE LAKE.

While here upon the banks of this small, but beautiful lake, the tourist will notice something of its loveliness. It is here that the Pemigewasset takes its rise. Starr King in describing it very properly remarks: "How much joy it has fed in human hearts! Something of its bounty expended upon the infant Pemigewasset is borne down into the Merrimac and contributes to the power that moves the wheels of Nashua and Lowell, and supplies a thousand operatives with bread." The lake is filled with the best of trout and affords sport for old fishermen.

ECHO LAKE.

A half mile north of the Profile House, and a fitting companion of Profile Lake, is another beautiful sheet of water—Echo Lake. It is a quiet and beautiful spot, and a ride upon its placid bosom, is indeed refreshing, after the fatigue of an all day ramble upon the adjacent mountains. But its great charm is in the wonderful echoes that reverberate among the mountain-fastnesses, on loud shouting, blowing of a horn, or firing of a cannon.

BALD MOUNTAIN.

Two miles north of the Profile House is Bald Mountain. A carriage road has been constructed to its summit and is now easy of access. From it is a fine view of the Ammonoosuc valley to the north, and to the south you look down upon Echo Lake and the Notch, while beyond rises Mt. Lafayette. Carriages run regularly from the hotel to the summit.

EAGLE CLIFF.

On the east side of the road leading through the

THE NOTCH FROM BALD MOUNTAIN.

Notch, opposite the Profile House, and completely overshadowing it, is Eagle Cliff. It rises 1,200 feet perpendicularly, and its peculiar formation makes it an object of interest to all. It derives its name from the fact, that some years since, a pair of eagles selected it for a home, and there reared their young.

CANNON MOUNTAIN.

In the rear and west of the Profile House, rising to the hight of 1,500 feet above the Notch, is Cannon Mountain. It receives its name from a rock upon the summit resembling a cannon, which can be seen from the grounds in front of the hotel. A foot-path, to the summit from the hotel, renders it comparatively easy of access. The view down the valley of the Pemigewasset is beautiful, and well repays the effort necessary to reach the summit. The view in other respects is fine, but not equal to that obtained from more elevated positions.

MT. LAFAYETTE.

Having visited the objects of general interest in the immediate vicinity of the Profile House, the tourist will ascend Mt. Lafayette, which is 5,000 feet in hight. The view from the summit is hardly inferior, and in some respects surpasses that from Mt. Washington. The distance from the hotel is five and a half miles. Careful guides and good ponies can be engaged at the hotel. On setting out for the trip, you proceed down the road, past the old Man of the Mountain, and for two miles follow the Pemigewasset. Coming to the site of the old Lafayette House, which was burned some years since, you turn to the left and enter the forest. Winding through it, you finally come out upon the bare rock, from which, you overlook the Profile House, down in the deep narrow glen. Further north is the valley of the Ammonoosuc. South, for twenty miles, you have full view of the lovely valley of the Pemigewasset and the river itself. After enjoying the view and resting your pony a few minutes, you continue the ascent. Finally coming out of the woods altogether, the bare and still distant peak of Lafayette lies before you. The summit seems so far above, you wonder how it is to be reached. Ploding on, zigzagging to right and left, the cone is finally gained. Such grandeur, as is spread before you, more than repays the toil necessary to reach the summit. Lofty mountain peaks without number, lie before you on every hand. West, in the hazy distance, is the Green Mountain range—Mt. Mansfield, Camel's Hump and Jay Peak towering above their neighbors. Intervening are the valleys of the Ammonoosuc and Connecticut. North is the glorious and grand old peak, Mt. Washington—the Tip Top House, if not cloud covered, in full view. Lying between are the summits of smaller mountains, while a trackless wilderness stretches far away towards the east, where peak upon peak rises skyward. A little to the left is old Kearsearge, and to the right the sharp spur of Chocorua seems to pierce the very sky. South, you look down upon the lovely valley of the Pemigewasset, which has seemingly widened into broad meadows, and forty miles distant, the eye rests upon Plymouth, and the beautiful Lake Winnipiseogee, with its innumerable islands. You linger long in contemplating the scene, and wonder how it is possible, that so much sublimity should remain so comparatively unknown to the great world of humanity within a day's ride, and yet so accessible. The summit of Mt. Lafayette is void of vegetation, and formerly a rude house stood upon it, for the protection of visitors. Time and the elements, however, have destroyed it. Ready to return, you look carefully to your saddle girths and set out for the hotel, where you arrive in season for dinner, having accomplished the whole trip, in about five hours.

DOWN THE PEMIGEWASSET.

Having rested from the fatigue occasioned by the ascent of Mt. Lafayette, the tourist is prepared to take a trip down the Pemigewasset, to see some of the objects of interest, that are found along this impetuous little stream, among which are the Basin, the Pool, the Flume, and Walker's and Georgianna Falls. The public carriages leave the hotel twice a day, at eight and a half a. m. and three p. m.

THE BASIN.

Four miles south of the Profile House, and on the west side of the road, is the Basin. The Pemigewasset in its downward course, flowing over a rocky ledge, has worn a complete basin out of the solid granite, sixty feet in circumference and about twenty feet in depth. In the outer edge, nearest the road, is a peculiar formation of granite, worn by the water and resembling the human foot and leg.

THE POOL.

Further south, and about five and a-half miles from the Profile House, is the Pool. You leave the carriage road just north of the old Flume House, and turn toward the east. A walk of half a mile through the forest will bring you to the Pool, which lies in the deep gorge between the mountains. The Pool is about forty feet deep, and 150 in width, and the Pemigewasset, entering at the upper side, has worn this huge cavern in the solid rock. Its grandeur is not so fully realized until the tourist has passed down the rude stairway to the bottom, where on either hand, the rocky sides rise above him, while the Pemigewasset itself rolls impetuously down from above, and thence out over the broken bed below. Here, too, in years past, has been found the "Philosopher," who is ready, with his boat, to take you, for a small stipend, around the pool, and give you his theory of its creation. Returning, you soon come to the site of the old Flume House, once a favorite place of resort.

THE FLUME.

Like the "Old Man of the Mountain," the Flume is one of the most important objects of interest, and no tourist should fail to visit it. The carriage leaves the road leading down the valley, just below where the old Flume House stood, and turns to the east. It crosses the Pemigewasset and halts a short distance below the Flume. "Leaving the wagon," says Starr King, "we mount by a footpath that leads nearer to the sweet melody that gives a promise to the ear, which is not to be broken to the hope. Soon we reach the clean and sloping granite floors, over which the water slips in thin, wide, even sheets of crystal colorlessness. Above this, we meet those gentle ripples over rougher ledges that are embossed with green. Then, still higher up, where the rocks grow more uneven, we are held by the profuse beauty of the hues shown upon the bright stones at the bottom of the little translucent basins and pools. Still above, we come to the remarkable fissure in the mountain, more than fifty feet high, and several

THE FLUME.—ABOVE THE BOULDER.

hundred feet long, which narrows, too, toward the upper end, till it only becomes only twelve feet wide, and which, doubtless, an earthquake made for the passage of the stream, which the visitors are now to ascend. We go up, stepping from rock to rock,—now walking along a little plank pathway, now mounting by some rude steps, here and there crossing from side to side of the ravine, by primitive little bridges, that bend under the feet, and that are railed by birch poles, and then climbing the rocks again, while the spray breaks upon us from the dashing and roaring stream, until we arrive at a little bridge which spans the narrowest part of the ravine. How wild the spot is! which shall we admire most—the glee of the little torrent that rushes beneath our feet, or the regularity and smoothness of the frowning walls through which it goes foaming out into the sunshine; or the splendor of the dripping emerald mosses; or the trees that overhang their edges; or the huge boulder, egg-shaped, that is lodged between the walls, just over the bridge where we stand—as unpleasant to look at, if the nerves are irresolute, as the sword of Damocles, and yet held by a grasp out of which it will not slip for centuries." Leaving the Flume, and following the foot-path above, along the northern side, you come to the rustic bridge which spans the chasm over the boulder. Here can be had an excellent view of the Flume, from one end to the other. It is a pleasant spot for meditation, and all nature around you seems in harmony. You are lost in wonder over the cause which produced such a remarkable scene. Whence came the power that rent these rocks asunder? and how long has this great granite boulder been suspended in its singular position?

The tourist has now seen the more important objects of interest in the Franconia Notch, but if he has time, he will find pleasure in taking other rambles among the mountains. On leaving the Flume and reaching the road, he can proceed down the valley for about two miles and then turn to the right, follow up a little stream, into the mountains, where he will come to Georgianna Falls, a series of beautiful cascades. Or, he can retrace his steps, and, when within about three miles of the Profile House, push into the woods, to the right, and come to Walker's Falls, where the little mountain stream makes a descent over an irregularly rocky bed.

FOR THE CRAWFORD HOUSE.

At eight and a-half, a. m., the coach is in readiness for the Crawford House, which is situated at the western entrance to the White Mountain Notch. You go back nearly to Franconia village by the same route you reached the Profile House from Littleton, and then turn to the right and proceed to

BETHLEHEM.

The scenery around Bethlehem is charming and beautiful. A distant view can be had of Mt. Washington and other peaks farther to the north.

LOWER AMMONOOSUC FALLS.

Leaving Bethlehem, where the coach stops for a few minutes, a ride of about two miles brings you to Ammonoosuc Bridge. Here Capt. Rosebrook built a bridge in the early settlement of Bethlehem. It was afterward carried away by high water, and, in 1800, the town of Bethlehem voted to build another at a cost of $390. Provisions were so scarce, that year, that the workmen were compelled to live on milk-porridge while building it. A short ride from this place brings you to Lower Ammonoosuc Falls, on the south side of the road. The Ammonoosuc is one of the wildest rivers in the State, and it makes a fall of about one mile in a distance of thirty miles, from the White Mountains to the Connecticut.

THE TWIN MOUNTAIN HOUSE.

The Railroad from Littleton to this place was completed sometime since, and now extends to Fabyan's, within five miles of the White Mountain Notch. This Hotel was built by A. T. & O. F. Barron, who keep the hotel at White River Junction and the Crawford House, at the White Mountain Notch. It has become a favorite place, and is within easy reach of the summit of Mt. Washington.

THE WHITE MOUNTAIN HOUSE.

Within five miles of Crawford's, is the White Mountain House, one of the oldest hotels in the mountain region. It is situated within full view Mt. Washington.

THE FABYAN HOUSE.

A half mile east of the White Mountain House is Fabyan's, the present terminus of the Railroad. Here was built, in 1803, the first public house kept in the White Mountains. From this place, in 1819, Ethan Allen Crawford, who lived here, and his father, Abel Crawford, who lived eight miles below the White Mountain Notch, cleared a path to the west side of Mt. Washington. Here was located that peculiar earth formation known as the Giant's

Grave; but which was leveled by the projector of the hotel. Three hotels, at various times, have been burned here, while the fields have been ravaged by freshets. The present hotel, the Fabyan House, was opened for guests in 1873, and is now one of the best hotels in the White Mountain region. It is kept by Lindsey, French & Co., well known landlords. Here, also, is the commencement of the White Mountain turnpike, which leads to the foot of the Mt. Washington Railway, six miles distant. Near here are the Ammonoosuc Falls, while within easy drive is the famous White Mountain Notch.

ARRIVAL AT CRAWFORD'S.

The Crawford House, four and a-half miles from the Fabyan House, is near the White Mountain Notch, a sight of which alone is sufficiently interesting to well repay the cost of the whole trip. From here you can go to the summit of Mt. Washington by ponies, or make the complete circuit of the mountains by stage. But before introducing you to the wild scenery of this locality, we will give you some preliminaries concerning the mountains themselves.

WHO NAMED THE MOUNTAINS.

The several peaks of the White Mountain range were named by a party from Lancaster, N. H., in 1820. Starr King, in his excellent book on the White Hills, who, by the way, did much in his lifetime, to make the public familiar with the beauty of this mountain region, very justly criticises the propriety of naming the mountains after the public men of the day. He says: "How absurd the order is! Beginning at 'The Notch,' at the Crawford House, and passing around to Gorham, these are the titles of the summits, which are all seen from the village of Lancaster: Webster, Clinton, Pleasant, Franklin, Monroe, Washington, Clay, Jefferson, Adams, and Madison. What a wretched jumble! These are what we have taken in exchange for such Indian words as Agiochook, which is the baptismal title of Mt. Washington, Ammonoosuc, Moosehillock, Cantoocook, Pennocook, and Pentucket. Think of putting Mount Monroe, or Peabody River, or Berlin Falls, or Israel's River, into poetry! The White Mountains have lost the privilege of being enshrined in such sonorous rythm and such melody as Longfellow has given to the Indian names in Hiawatha."

THE HIGHT OF THE DIFFERENT PEAKS.

Below is the hight, above the sea, of the several peaks of the White Mountain range, of which Mt. Washington is the highest:

Mt. Webster,	4,000 feet.	Mt. Washington,	6,285 feet.
" Jackson,	4,100 "	" Clay,	5,400 "
" Clinton,	4,200 "	" Jefferson,	5,700 "
" Pleasant,	4,800 "	" Adams,	5,800 "
" Franklin,	4,900 "	" Madison,	5,400 "
" Monroe,	5,400 "		

THE CRAWFORD HOUSE.

The Crawford House is situated on a broad plateau, 2,000 feet above the sea, at the Western entrance to the White Mountain Notch, twenty-two miles from Littleton, and thirty-five miles, by stage route, from the Glen House, on the eastern side of the mountains. The Hotel stands on the watershed between the Saco and the Connecticut—the water at the barn, just west of the Hotel, running west into the Ammonoosuc, and then into the Connecticut; while that, a little east of the Hotel runs into the Saco. The Hotel is spacious, and is pleasantly furnished, and its proprietors, the Messrs. Barron, spare no pains to provide for the wants of their guests. A band of music is kept at the Hotel during the season, and at night, after the return of visitors from their day's tramp among the mountains, the elegantly furnished parlor is the center of a gay scene. Fatigued though the tourist may be, a new life and vigor is at once infused, as the inspiring music falls upon the ear.

MT. WILLARD.

If the tourist came by the morning coach, he will have ample time, after dinner, to visit Mt. Willard and the Notch. The former is only two miles from the Hotel, and a good carriage road has been constructed to its summit. Frequently, tourists who were never before here, thinking this to be of no particular interest, neglect to visit it. No where in the whole mountains is a finer and more striking view had, and no one should fail of seeing it. The Hotel carriage will be in readiness, after dinner, to make the trip. Leaving the Crawford House, you go a short distance east, down the road toward the Notch, when you turn to the right and enter the woods. The road is generally good, and, with few exceptions, is not steep. Making a somewhat circuitous ascent, you finally come out upon a plateau, where a most sublime scene bursts upon you. Two thousand feet below lies the famous White Mountain Notch, so narrow that there is only little more than room enough for the Saco river and the carriage road. The forest of spruce seem like low shrubs, while the famous Willey House, half way down the Notch, is only discernable. On the right is Mt. Willard, and, on the left, Mt. Webster, their deep furrowed walls showing plainly the many slides that have taken place here in times past. You approach the edge of the precipice and sit down upon the bare rock and contemplate the scene. You look down the deep gorge, and beyond, to the distant mountain peaks, or note, by the growth of the shrubbery, the spot where the great avalanche swept down Mt. Willey, and buried the Willeys beneath it. A visit to this place in the afternoon is preferable. The west side is covered with a deep shadow, while, on the east, the golden sun-light still lingers on Mt. Webster, giving the scene a picturesque appearance. Leaving the place reluctantly, you resume your seat in the coach, and return to the Hotel.

DOWN THE NOTCH.

There is still time left for a visit to the famous Willey House, three miles distant, in the White Mountain Notch. Leaving the Hotel and traveling eastward, you come to the Source of the Saco, a little pond just to the left of the road, and in view of the Crawford House. Here, this river, which becomes a stream of considerable importance before reaching the ocean, is only a little trickling rivulet. Passing on, and just before you reach the entrance to the Notch, you will notice, on the left, Elephant's Head, a huge rock, so named from the fact, that it resembles the head and trunk of a mammoth elephant. While viewing this, as we

THE WHITE MOUNTAIN NOTCH.

pass, we are "reminded of a little story." Some time since, a very devout gentleman, who had come to the mountains with the Good Book in one pocket and a Guide Book in the other, and, like a good man, as he was, having that morning read both, names and places were a "little mixed." He accosted our jolly driver with: "Can you tell me, driver, where is Ephraim's Head?" "Ephraim's Head? You have the start of me, now, sir! Guess there's no such place about these mountains." "Yes, there must be, I read about it this morning." "Don't you mean Elephant's Head?" The good man drew forth his guide book to make sure that he was right, and was afterward seen quietly replacing it in his pocket, remarking, as he did so, something about poor "specs" and bad eyesight.

THE GATEWAY.

Passing on, you enter the Gateway to the Notch. The Saco finds its way through the rocks at your side, while, almost perpendicularly, rise above you, in curious forms, great masses of rocks, in almost every conceivable shape. The driver, who is not deficient in imagination, will point out various profiles, from the little infant to the old maid. A little further on you come to

FLUME AND SILVER CASCADES,

both of which come dashing down over the irregular and rocky surface of Mt. Webster, on your left. The Flume Cascade, which you first reach, is more regular and less interesting than Silver Cascade. The latter makes a descent of more than four hundred feet, and, as it leaps from rock to rock, it presents an extremely enchanting appearance. It seems like a silver cord stretching up toward the very clouds.

THE DEVIL'S DEN.

As you pass down the Notch, the driver will point out to your view the summit of Mt. Willard, and on its broken face, a cavern in the rock. This is the Devil's Den, though we have some doubts concerning its occupancy by his satanic majesty. This cavern is only accessible by means of ropes from the summit of Mt. Willard. Dr. Ball, of Boston, explored it in 1856, and found it to be twenty feet wide, fifteen high, and twenty feet deep. A better view can be had of it as you come up the Notch.

THE WILLEY HOUSE.—THE TERRIBLE DISASTER.

Continuing down the Notch, you at last come to the Willey House, made famous by that terrible calamity that happened here more than forty years ago. It stands on the west side of the road, Mt. Willey rising from its rear to the hight of 2000 feet. The original house (an addition has since been erected, adjoining it on the south) was built for a public house by a Mr. Hill, about the year 1820, who occupied it for one year. Before it was built, there was no house for thirteen miles, from the old Crawford place, south of the Willey House, to Rose-brook's, near the Giant's Grave. In the Autumn of 1825, Mr. James Willey, Jr., moved into the house and on the night of August 28, 1826, a terrible storm raged in the Notch, masses of rocks, trees and earth, covering a space of nearly a mile in length, were precipitated from the side of Mt. Willey into the valley below, burying the whole family, consisting of nine persons, Mr. Willey and wife, five children and two hired men. Mr. Willey apprehending that a slide might take place, had constructed a rude hut below the house to which, he thought his family might retreat with safety, in case of necessity. It appears that some time during the night, his family set out to reach the hut, and were overtaken and buried in the advancing avalanche. A huge rock thirty feet high, stood in the rear of the house, which parted the sliding mass and saved the building from destruction. Had the family remained in it, their lives would have been saved.

Starr King has told the story of this terrible tragedy so admirably in his White Hills, that we transfer it to these pages. He says: "In the Spring of 1826, Mr. Willey began to enlarge the convenience of the little inn for entertaining guests. There was a beautiful meadow in front stretching to the foot of the frowning wall of Mount Webster, and garrisoned with tall rock maples. To be sure, Mount Willey rose at a rather threatening angle some two thousand feet behind the house, but it was not so savage in appearance as Mt. Webster opposite, and pretty much the whole of its broad steep wall was draped in green. In a bright June morning the little meadow farm, flecked with the nibbling sheep, and cooled by the patches of shadow flung far out over the grass from the thick maple foliage, must have seemed to a traveler passing there, and hearing the pleasant murmur of the Saco and the shrill sweetness of the Canada whistler, as romantic a spot as one could fly to, to escape the fever and the perils of the world."

Late in June Mr. Willey and his wife, looking from

the back windows of their house, in the afternoon of a misty day, saw a large mass of the mountain above them sliding through the fog towards their meadows, and almost in a line of the house itself. Rocks and earth came plunging down, sweeping whole trees before them, that would stand erect in the swift slide for rods before they fell. The slide moved under their eye to the very foot of the mountain, and hurled its frightful burden across the road. At first they were greatly terrified and resolved to move from the Notch. But Mr. Willey, on reflection, felt confident that such an event was not likely to occur again; and was satisfied with building a strong hut or cave a little below the house in the Notch, which would certainly be secure, and to which the family might fly for shelter. Later in the summer there was a long hot drought. By the middle of August, the earth, to a great depth in the mountain region, was dried to powder. There came several days of south wind, betokening copious rain. On Sunday, the 27th of August, the rain began to fall. On Monday, the 28th, the storm was very severe, and the rain was a deluge. Towards evening the clouds around the White Mountain range and over the Notch, to those who saw them from a distance, were heavy, black and awful. Later in the night they poured their burden in streams. Between nine o'clock in the evening and the dawn of Tuesday, the Saco rose twenty-five feet, and swept the whole interval between the Notch and Conway. On the morning of Tuesday the sun rose into a cloudless sky, and the air was remarkably transparent The North Conway farmers, busy in saving what they could from the raging flood of the Saco, saw clearly how terrible the storm had been upon the White Mountain range. The whole line was devastated by land-slides. Great grooves could be distinctly seen, where the torrents had torn all the loose earth and stones and left the solid ledge of the mountain bare. What had been the fate of the little house in the Notch, and the Willey family during the deluge? All communication with them on Tuesday morning was cut off by the flood of the Saco. But at four o'clock Tuesday afternoon, a traveler passing Ethan Crawford's, seven miles west of the Willey House, desired if possible to get through the Notch that night. By swimming his horse across the wildest part of the flood, he was put on the track. In the narrowest part of the road within the Notch, the warter had torn out huge rocks and left holes twenty feet deep, and had opened trenches also ten feet deep and twenty feet long. But the traveler, while daylight lasted, could make his way on foot over the torn and obstructed road, and he reached the lower part of the Notch just before dark. The little house was standing, but there was no human inmates to greet him. And what desolation around! The mountain behind it, once robed in beautiful green, was striped for two or three miles with ravines, deep and freshly torn. The lovely little meadow in front was covered with wet sand and rocks, intermingled with branches of green trees, with shivered trunks whose splintered ends looked similar to an old peeled birchbroom, and with dead logs, which had evidently long been buried beneath the mountain soil. Not even any of the bushes that grew up on the meadow in front of the house were to be seen. The slide from the mountain had evidently divided, not many rods above the house, against a sharp ledge of rock. It had then joined the frightful mass in front of the house, and pushed along to the bed of the Saco, covering the meadow, in some places, thirty feet, with the frightful debris and mire. The traveler entered the house and went through it. The doors were all open; the beds and their clothing showed that they had been hurriedly left; a Bible was lying open on a table, as if it had been read just before the family had departed. The traveler consoled himself, at last, with the feeling that the inmates had escaped to Abel Crawford's below, and then tried to sleep in one of the deserted beds. But in the night he heard moanings, which frightened him so much, he lay sleepless till dawn. Then he found that they were the groans of an ox in the stable, that was partly crushed under broken timbers which had fallen in. The two horses were killed. He released the ox and went on his way towards Bartlett. Before any news of the disaster had reached Conway, the faithful dog came down to Mr. Lovejoy's, and, by moanings, tried to make the family understand what had taken place. Not succeeding, he left, and after being seen frequently on the road, sometimes heading north and then south running almost at the top of his speed, as though bent on some absorbing errand, he soon disappeared from the region, and has never since been seen. On Wednesday evening suspicions of the safety of the family were carried down to Bartlett and North Conway, where Mr. Willey's father and brothers lived. But they were not credited. The terrible certainty was to be communicated to the father in a most thrilling way. At midnight on Wednesday, a messenger reached the bank of the river opposite his house in Lower Bartlett, but could not cross. He blew a trumpet, blast after blast. The noise and the mountain echoes startld the family and the neighborhood from their repose. They soon gathered on the river bank and heard the sad message shouted to them through the darkness. On Thursday, the 31st of August, the family and many neighbors were able to reach the Notch. Search was commenced at once for the buried bodies. The first that was exhumed was one of the hired men, David Allen, a man of powerful frame and remarkable strength. He was but slightly disfigured. He was found near the top of a pile of earth and shattered timbers, with hands clenched and full of broken sticks and small limbs of trees. Soon the bodies of Mrs. Willey and her husband were discovered—the latter not so crushed that it could not be recognized. No more could be found that day. Rude coffins were prepared, and the next day, Friday, about sunset, the simple burial service was offered. Elder Samuel Hasaltine, standing admist the company of strong, manly forms, where faces were wet with tears, commenced the service with the words of Isaiah: "Who hath measured the waters in the hollow of his hand, and meted out heaven with a span, and comprehended the dust of the earth in a measure, and weighed the mountains in scales, and the hills in a balance?" How fitting this language in that solemn pass, and how unspeakably more impressive must the words have seemed, when the mountains themselves took them up, and literally responded them, joining as mourners in the burial liturgy! For the minister stood so that each one of these sublime words was given back by the echo, in a tone as clear and reverent as that in which they were uttered. The next day the body of the youngest child, about three years old, was found, and also that of the other hired man. On Sunday, the eldest daughter was discovered, at a distance from the others, across the river. A bed was found on the ruins near her body. It was supposed that she was drowned, as no bruise or mark was found upon her. She was twelve years old, and Ethan Crawford tells us, had acquired a good education, and seemed more like a gentleman's daughter of fashion and affluence, than a daughter of one who had located himself in the midst of the mountains. These were buried without any religious service. Three children—a daughter and two sons—were never found. The relatives who studied the ground closely after the disaster, were unable to conjecture why the family could not have outrun the landslide, or crossed its track, if they left the house as soon as they heard its descent up the mountain. Some of them, at least, they thought, should thus have been able to escape its devastation. Mr. James Willey informs us, that the spirit of his brother appeared to him in a dream, and told him that the family left the house sometime before the avalanche, fearing to be drowned, or floated off by the Saco, which had risen to the door. They fled back, he said, further up the mountain to be safe against the peril of water, and thus, when the landslide moved towards them, were compelled to run a greater distance to escape it than would have been required if they had stayed in their home; while they would have been swept off by the flood, if they had kept the line of the road which would have conducted them out of the Notch. It is a singular fact, Mr. Benjamin Willey tells us, that this explanation accounts for more known features of the catastrophe than any other which has been found. It explains why the eldest daughter was found without a bruise as though she had been drowned; and also the fact that a bed was found near her body, with which certainly the family would not have encumbered themselves, if they had rushed from the house with the single hope of escaping destruction when the avalanche was near. It accounts for the appearance of the body of the hired man, who was first discovered. And by connecting the terror of a sudden flood with the other horrors of the night, it brings the picture into harmony with what we know of the ravage and disaster along the

Saco below. The Bible was open on the table in the Willey House when it was entered the next day. The family were then secure from the wrath of elements that desolate the earth. At what place could the book have been found open more fitting than the sixteenth Psalm, to express the horrors of the tempest and the deliverance which the spirit finds? "The Lord also thundered in the heavens, and the Highest gave his voice; hailstones and coals of fire. Then the channels of waters were seen, and the foundations of the world were discovered at thy rebuke, O Lord, at the blast of the breath of thy nostrils. He sent from above, he took me, he drew me out of many waters. He brought me forth also into a large place; he delivered me, because he delighted in me." South of the Willey House, upon the spot where a portion of the family were buried by the avalanche, it was a custom during several years, for each visitor to cast a stone, and thus a large monumnet was reared out of the ruins of the slide.

RETURN TO THE CRAWFORD HOUSE.—THE NOTCH IN FORMER DAYS.

After the carriage has taken the tourist to the monument south of the Willey House, it returns to the Hotel. The view as you pass up the Notch is more interesting than the one you get while going down. The bare and broken rocks on the side of Mt. Willard stand before you like a great wall. In the early settlement of New Hampshire, a turnpike was constructed through the Notch at a cost of $40,-

ooo, and until the railroads were built, there was a great deal of travel through it, to and from Portsmouth. The Notch was discovered in 1772, by a hunter named Nash, who climbed a tree on Cherry Mountain, west of the Crawford House. It was, however, with great difficulty that teams could pass through it. Horses were pulled up the narrowest portions between Mt. Willey and Mt. Webster, and let down by ropes. "The primitive method," says Starr King, "of transporting any commodities, was to cut two poles some fifteen feet in length, nail a couple of bars across the middle, on which a bag or barrel could be fastened, then harness the horse into the smaller ends, which served as thills, and let the larger ends, which had no wheels under them, drag on the ground. The first article of commerce that was carried in this way from the sea-shore, through the solemn walls and over the splintered outlet of the Notch, was a barrel of rum. It was taxed heavily in its own substance, however, to ensure its passage, and reached the Ammonoosuc Meadows, west of the Notch, in a very reduced condition."

BEECHER'S CASCADE.

In the rear of the Crawford House is Beecher's Cascade. Formerly this was known as Gibbs' Falls, named after a former proprietor of the Hotel. Mr. Gibbs' name has been attached to another, in the woods on the opposite side of the road. Leaving the Hotel you turn to the right and enter the footpath along side of the small mountain stream. In a few minutes you come to the first cascade. Here

Henry Ward Beecher took an involuntary bath, and since, his name has been given to the pretty little water-fall. For nearly half a mile up the mountain you will find a series of small cascades quite pretty to look upon. Cross the stream and follow the foot-path near it, until you come at last to the guide-board pointing north. Here upon this rock a beautiful view is to be had. Looking out through the opening in the forest, you have a good view of Mt. Washington and the Tip-Top House on its summit. This is the only place near the Crawford House, accessible by foot-path, where a view of Mt. Washington can be had. It is a quiet, charming place, and all will enjoy the walk to it as well as the view.

THE MT. WILLEY CASCADES.

There are several cascades on Mt. Willey, seldom visited by tourists, that are said to be quite equal to any in the mountain region. They were first discovered in 1858. To reach them you go down the Notch until you come to Cow Brook, the second stream below the Willey House. Following this for nearly two miles into the mountains, you come to Sylvan Glade Cataract. Here the little stream leaps down a rocky stairway and then glides down a solid bed of granite, 150 feet at an angle of 45 degrees. A mile higher is Sparkling Cascade, quite equal in beauty to the first. Some labor is necessary to reach these water-falls, but if one has the leisure he will find himself well repaid.

THROUGH THE NOTCH TO THE GLEN HOUSE.

Until the Mt. Washington Railway was built, the

travel from the Crawford to the Glen House, on the east side of Mt. Washington, was by stage, mostly through the White Mountain Notch, though tourists frequently went over Cherry Mountain to the Waumbeek House, at Jefferson, and thence to the Glen. The view of the White Mountains from this route is very fine. But we will now pass down the Notch to the Willey House, and thence to the Old Abel Crawford place, a half mile below. Abel Crawford, who lived here, was the pioneer of all this region, and Daniel Webster and other distinguished men were his guests, long before the tide of pleasure travel had set in this direction. The Railroad, which has been approaching the Notch, has at last reached this point, and, before long, pleasure seekers will ride through to the Crawford House, direct from Boston and Portland, coming up the valley by North Conway.

NANCY'S BROOK.

Below the old Crawford place is Nancy's Brook. A poor girl, who lived with a family at Jefferson, was found frozen to death here in 1778. She was engaged to be married to a man who lived in the same family, and to whom she had intrusted all her earnings. They were to leave for Portsmouth in a few days, to be married, and while she was absent in Lancaster, the faithless lover started for Portsmouth with his employer, without leaving any explanation for her. She learned the fact the day he left, and at once walked nine miles, to Jefferson, where she tied up a small bundle, and started in pursuit. Snow had fallen, and only a hunter's path, marked by spotted trees, indicated the way through the wilderness. It was thirty miles to the Notch, but, nothing daunted, she set out at nightfall, hoping to overtake her lover in camp at the Notch, before the party left next morning. When she reached the spot, they had left, though the ashes of the campfire were still warm. Continuing down through the Notch, where only one woman had passed before her, cold, wet, and hungry, she sank exhausted by the side of a tree near "Nancy's Brook." Alarmed for her safety, a party left Jefferson in pursuit, and found her, chilled and stiff, in the snow, her head resting upon her staff, not a long time after she had ceased to breath. The lover of the poor girl, on hearing the story of her faithfulness, her suffering, and death, became insane, and died a raving maniac.

SAWYER'S ROCK.

Below Nancy's Brook is Sawyer's Rock. The discovery of the Notch by a hunter named Nash, who climbed a tree on Cherry Mountain, was made known to Governor Wentworth. The Governor promised Nash a large tract of land if he would demonstrate the feasibility of the pass by bringing a horse through it to Portsmouth. Aided by a fellow-hunter named Sawyer, the horse was let down the rocks, at various places, until they had passed over all. Draining his rum bottle and dashing it on the rock, Sawyer exclaimed, "This shall hereafter be called Sawyer's Rock!" Just below the

Rock you come to Upper Bartlett. From here to Ellis River, the Saco valley is more broad and fertile. On reaching Ellis River you turn to the left, and pursue a more northerly route to Jackson. From Jackson to the Glen House, you pass through Pinkham Notch. The scenery is quite interesting, the mountains rising to a great hight.

GLEN ELLIS FALLS.

Four miles south of the Glen House is Glen Ellis Falls. You leave the carriage and enter the woods on the east side, and a walk of a few minutes brings you to the grandest cataract in the White Mountain region. The Ellis River, in its southward course, is here compressed into a narrow channel, and, at this point, makes almost a perpendicular descent of sixty feet at a single bound. You should pass down the stair-way, to the bottom of the fall, to get its greatest beauty. An hour spent here in studying the wildness of the scenery will always be a pleasing recollection of your visit to the White Mountains.

CRYSTAL CASCADE.

Continuing up the Glen till you come to the guide board, three miles from the hotel, you leave the carriage and follow the foot-path for nearly half an hour, when you come to Crystal Cascade. Part of the water comes from the summit of Mt. Washington, through Tuckerman's Ravine. Stopping for a moment at the bottom to view the cascade, you climb to the top of the high bank opposite, that overhangs it, where a better view is had. Is there anything more beautiful? At the top the water issues from among the rocks in a single narrow stream, and its descent broadens until it reaches the pool below. One writer has very happily compared it "to an inverted liquid plume—the rill above, where the water is one stream, being the stem, and the widening, fleecy flow its nodding, graceful, feathery spray."

THE GLEN HOUSE.

This has long been one of the famous places in the White Mountains. Down in the narrow valley, between Mt. Washington and Mt. Carter, is the Glen House. The Mt. Carter range, east of the Hotel, is 3,000 feet high, while on the west, rises Mts.

Washington, Clay, Jefferson, Adams and Madison, to almost twice that hight. This is only eight miles from the Alpine House, at Gorham. This place was made famous by J. M. Thompson, long its landlord. He was drowned, several years since, while in his sawmill, which was carried off by a sudden rise in the river. It is now kept by W. & R. Milliken. There are several other minor points of interest in this vicinity; but the carriage road to the summit of Mt. Washington has made this, in the past, a favorite place of resort.

THE ASCENT OF MT. WASHINGTON.

Long before the carriage road from the Glen House, on the east side, to the summit of Mt. Washington, and the Railway, on the west side, were built, the ascent was made on horseback, by the bridle-paths to the summit. The ride from the Crawford House, over the cone of the several mountain peaks, was of great interest, though fatiguing. Later improvements have done away, in a great measure, with this sort of travel. The first was the building of the

MOUNT WASHINGTON CARRIAGE ROAD.

This is one of the greatest triumphs of engineering skill. Commencing in front of the Glen House, it was made over a circuitous route to the Tip-Top House, on the cone of Mount Washington. Its entire length is eight miles, and no where does its grade exceed sixteen feet in one hundred, while its average is only twelve. It is broad and well built, and no where is there a better road in New England.

A charter was procured, and, in 1855, its construction was commenced, under the management of Mr. D. O. Macomber. In the following year it was finished to the Ledge, four miles from the Glen House. Five years afterward, in 1861, it was completed to the summit, and opened for travel. The surveys were made and the road laid out by Mr. Charles H. V. Cavis, who continued to be Superintendent of construction until 1857, when work was suspended on account of financial difficulties. For half the way up the mountain the road winds through the forest, coming out at the Ledge. From here it continues along the edge of the deep ravine, which separates Mount Washington from Jefferson and Adams. Then it curves to the eastern side of the mountain, where it overlooks Peabody and Ellis Rivers. The scenery here is, perhaps, superior to that of any other part of the road. Above and below you can see the carriages moving slowly along the road, while the distant view is grand in the extreme. Just before reaching the summit, you will notice, on your right, the rude monument which marks the spot where Miss Bourne died of exhaustion, in September, 1855. The ascent is made in four hours, by the carriages, from the Glen House.

THE MOUNT WASHINGTON RAILWAY.

The Mount Washington Railway, projected by Sylvester Marsh, of Littleton, and completed in 1869, has made the ascent of Mount Washington much less difficult, and thousands now visit its summit who have hitherto regarded it as almost impossible. The road is located upon the west side of the mountain, near the old Fabyan path, commencing at a point six miles from the Fabyan House, and at an elevation of about twelve hundred feet above it. The railroad is nearly three miles long, and overcomes an elevation of 3,606 feet. Its sharpest grade is nearly one foot in three, and its least, one foot in ten. The third, or center rail, is fitted with a series of cogs, in which the gearing of the engine and car work, walking, as it were, up the mountain. The ascent is made in an hour and a-half, and with perfect safety. The engine and car weigh about twelve tons, and a cord of wood and thirty barrels of water are necessary to make the trip. The railroad and rolling stock have cost $200,000, and are used only about eight weeks in the year. Mr. Marsh is entitled to great credit for starting the project; but Mr. Walter Aiken, of Franklin, N. H., has been the practical man, to take hold and complete the work. He built the engines, and carried forward the railway to completion. He is a thorough mechanic, and is entitled to great praise.

Leaving the Crawford, Fabyan, or Twin Mountain Houses, in the morning, by stage, the station is reached in season to make the ascent at 10.30. The car will seat about fifty persons, and is pushed slowly and steadily up the mountain till the summit is gained, an hour and a-half after starting. As the ascent is continued, the valley below seems to be receding, while the distant mountain peaks come slowly into view. If the weather is favorable, the ascent is, in every respect, delightful. The overheated atmosphere is exchanged for that which is cool and invigorating. Halting, for a few moments, to take in water, the ascent is continued, and you pass the Lizzie Bourne monument, made of rude stones, just before reaching the hotel. At last, you make the final stop in front of the Summit House,

three miles from the base, and an hour and a-half after starting. This is on the cone of Mount Washing-

THE MOUNT WASHINGTON RAILROAD.

ton, 6291 feet above the level of the sea. Here you are at last, with the grandeur and beauty of all New England at your feet. Words fail to give adequate expression to the feeling that comes over you, as you stand in mute silence before this awe-inspiring scene. You may have read of grand old mountains, but nothing has pictured such vastness and sublimity. The scene is so grand and so vast, that you seem bewildered. Below, on every side, are huge mountain peaks, the earth's surface seemingly having been tossed into a tempest. A great cloud may sweep by, covering the summit in an almost impenetrable mist. In a few moments it has passed, and you are looking down upon a grand scene—the mountain peaks protruding through the thick clouds, resembling islands in a great lake. The dark and somber shadows of the mountains are beautifully mingled with the rose-tinted clouds that sweep by in the valleys below, made gorgeous by the rays of the setting sun. Can there be anything more beautiful to look upon than this ever-changing and never-ending scene? It quickens man's better nature and calls forth those feelings that are in harmony with the Great Spirit which pervades everything pure and beautiful.

The summit is made up of a broken mass of dark mica slate, so rough that you walk over it with great difficulty. Here is the large and commodious Summit House, kept by Capt. J. W. Dodge, the old Tip-Top and Summit Houses, and the United States Signal Service building. North, and near at hand, are Mts. Clay, Jefferson, Adams, and Madison. In the distance, beyond, are numberless peaks, and, rising from the northern forests of Maine is Mount Katahdin, 160 miles away. Easterly, and close at hand, are the Androscoggin River and valley, and Carter and Pinkham Notches, with the Glen House in full view. Beyond is the Carter Range, lakes, and innumerable mountain peaks. Further beyond is the harbor of Portland, easily seen in favorable weather. Lovewell's and Walker's ponds, and Sebago lake are easily seen, while Mount Kearsarge stands prominently in the foreground. In looking south, your eye falls upon the beautiful Saco valley at North Conway, a charming spot for rest and recu-

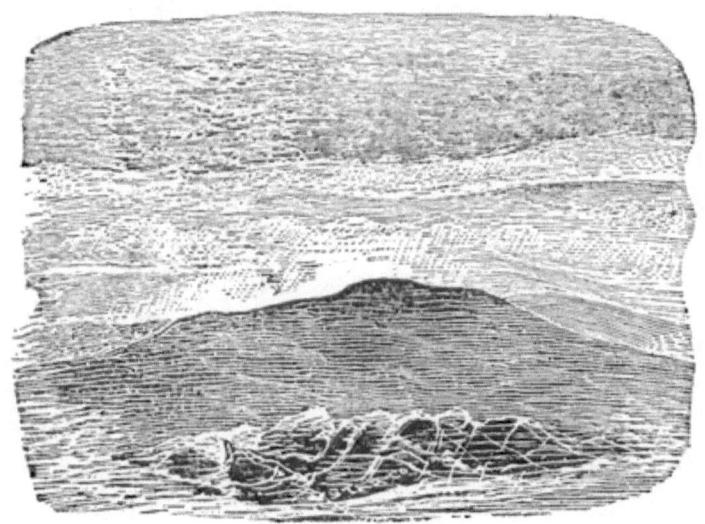

CLOUD VIEW FROM MT. WASHINGTON.

peration. The sharp and peculiarly formed peak of Chocorua forms a central figure in the southern view. It is a grand old mountain, and its peak seems almost to touch the sky. To the right is Lake Winnipisoegee, with its many islands, while, still beyond, are the dim outlines of Monadnock. Still farther to the right are Mts. Lafayette and Carrigan. Close by, and part of the White Mountain range, are Mts. Monroe, Franklin, Pleasant, and Clinton, over and along which is the old path to the Crawford House, now seldom used. West lies the beautiful Ammonoosuc valley, and beyond are the Green Mountains and the Adirondacks. These are some of the more prominent objects to be seen from Mt. Washington. The minor details, that fill the eye on every side, have a thousand beauties peculiar to themselves, and the tourist will need time to carefully study them to fully comprehend all that lies before him. The lights and shades as they alternate, reveal the hidden beauty of this great expanse, and so frequent and so many are the changes, that you never grow weary in tracing the deep valleys and the lofty mountain ranges as the beautiful clouds flit over them.

Close to the Summit House and easterly of it is Tuckerman's Ravine, named for Prof. Edward Tuckerman, who explored it years ago to complete his knowledge of the lichens and flora of the White Mountain region. It is nearly a mile from the summit to the bottom, and here the snow remains nearly through the year, disappearing in August, only a few weeks before it falls again.

Near the Railway, just north of the Summit House is the Lizzie Bourne monument, a rude pile of stones made to mark the spot where Miss Lizzie Bourne of Kennebunk perished in September, 1855. She with an uncle and cousin, left the Glen House in the afternoon of a lovely September day to walk on the carriage road, and tempted by the favorable weather they concluded to make the ascent of the mountain. Sunset and a deep fog settled over them and the wind became fierce and cutting, and finally Miss Bourne sank exhausted, about ten o'clock, within hailing distance of the summit. A wall of stone was thrown up to protect her against the wind, but she soon expired. Her friends remained with her until morning, which revealed to them the nearness of the Tip Top House. Not far from this place Benjamin Chandler, of Delaware, was lost, and his remains were not found for more than a year. Still farther below Dr. Hall of Boston, passed two nights in an October snow storm, without food or covering. His feet were frozen, but he was saved from death.

THE UNITED STATES SIGNAL STATION.

The United States Government established a Signal Station on Mt. Washington, in the autumn of 1871. It had a corps of observers on the mountain during the previous winter, with J. H. Huntington, who, with a small party went there and remained through the winter for the purpose of making observations. The station is in charge of Sergeant A. R. Thornett, who has two assistants, Sergeant William Lane and another gentleman. Sergeant Thornett is completing his third year. Observations are made daily, at 8 a. m., 5 and 11.30, p. m., and the result is sent to Washington by telegraph. Since observations have been taken at this station, the wind has blown, at its highest rate, 138 miles per hour, and the temperature has fallen as low as

55° below zero. A decrease of pressure here, as indicated by the barometer, is followed by a decrease of temperature and an increase of wind.

THE SUMMIT HOUSE.

Mr. Aiken and Mr. Lyon, who are the largest individual stockholders in the Mt. Washington Railway, have completed a large and commodious hotel on the summit of Mt. Washington, at the terminus of the Railway, capable of accommodating over two hundred guests. It is kept by Capt. J. W. Dodge, who also has charge of the Railway. The Captain keeps an excellent hotel and makes his guests at home. The house is heated by steam and whatever the weather may be at the summit, everything is comfortable and pleasant within. There is one thing that the tourist should not forget to take with him when he goes to the summit of Mt. Washington and that is, a contented spirit. The weather is always changeable. It may be pleasant when he arrives, and within half an hour the summit may be cloud-capped, completely cutting off the view. The only way is to wait patiently and in time the view will more than pay for the temporary disappointment. There is nothing more beautiful than the view below, as the clouds pass and reveal the many beautiful mountain peaks and valleys that lie on every side. Words cannot describe the emotions that come to those, who are thus privileged. The scene is too grand and too vast to be adequately described upon the printed page—it must be seen and felt to be understood.

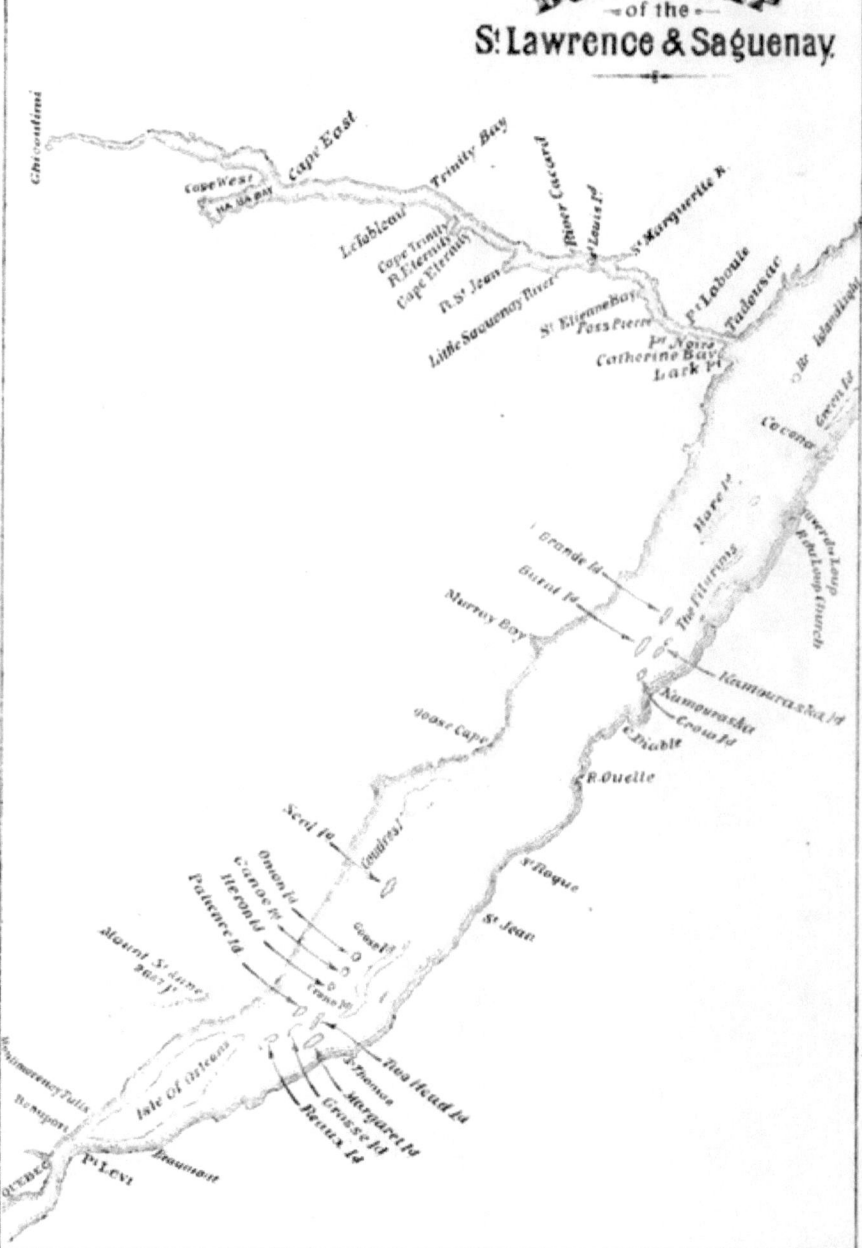

QUEBEC.

New York, 555; Boston, 395; Montreal, 180; Tadousac, 140; Ha! Ha! Bay, 200 miles.

St. John's Gate—as it was.

QUEBEC, famous in the early history of this Continent, and picturesquely situated, is a city of rare interest to those who have leisure to study its many peculiarities. Set down here for the first time at night, the morning would reveal such strange scenes, that one would hardly realize that he was still upon the Western Continent. The habits of the people, the peculiar style of architecture, and the varied street scenes, would more than half convince him that he had been transported to some old town in Continental Europe. Everything is unmistakably European. The people are slow and easy, and altogether lack that brisk, go-ahead spirit which distinguishes every American,—always so full of activity and enterprise. The history of Quebec dates back more than three centuries, and the customs of the early French settlers have been little changed during the time, though the government long ago passed from their hands and direction. The English have really made so little change, that the great tenacity of the French to preserve their own habits is everywhere apparent. They have been much larger in numbers than the English, or they are remarkable for resisting the influences of association.

Jacques Cartier, the celebrated navigator of St. Malo, in France, was the first white man to set foot upon this spot. In 1535 he left France on his second voyage of discovery, in search of a north-west passage to China. Mistaking the mouth of the St. Lawrence for the object of his search, he sailed up the river till he reached Stadacona, an Indian village on St. Charles river, just north of the promontory on which Quebec now stands, where he remained a short time before proceeding to Montreal, then an Indian settlement, and known as Hochelaga. Quebec, though discovered by Cartier, was founded by Champlain, in 1608, the Agent of a company of Merchants who had decided to establish settlements in Canada. The base of Cape Diamond, upon which upper Quebec now stands, was selected as the site of the first settlement in New France. That event occurred on the 3d of July, 1608, and this was, really, the beginning of French power in the New World, which, in the main, continued upward of a century and a-half. The

QUEBEC FROM POINT LEVI.

Jesuits came here and established churches, and their influence is felt here to this day. It was taken by the English in 1629, and restored to France by the Treaty of 1632. In 1759 the English Gen. Wolfe attacked the city and bombarded it, and on the 13th of September, the fist battle of the Plains of Abraham took place. His opponent was Gen. Montcalm, commander of the French forces; and, after a sanguinary encounter, both the contending generals fell, but the English were victorious, and thus was gained to England an American empire. Wolfe first took possession of the Isle of Orleans, and occupied Point Levi with a detachment. His able opponent, Gen. Montcalm, had thrown up entrenchments near the Falls of Montmorency. Gen. Moncton constructed batteries at Point Levi, and bombarded the town. The red-hot balls soon set fire to the buildings, and the lower town was destroyed. Gen. Wolfe became restive, and was eager for an attack on Montcalm's forces at Beauport, easterly of Quebec. This his generals disapproved. On the 12th of September, Capt. Cook, the great navigator, was sent to sound the waters off Beauport, as if an attack, in that quarter, was contemtemplated. Little after midnight Wolfe, with Moncton and Murray, set off in boats, and floated silently with the ebb tide till they reached the cove just west of the Plains of Abraham, where they disembarked and ascended the steep bank to the plains above. At daylight Wolfe stood at the head of his army on the Plains of Abraham. Bofore ten o'clock the two contending armies stood opposite each other, and, for two hours a fierce conflict raged. Wolfe had received two slight wounds, and, just as the fortunes of the day were turning in his favor, a third ball struck him in the breast, and, while in the agonies of death, he heard the cry of "They flee." When, on being told that it was the French who fled, he exclaimed, "Now God be praised, I die happy!" Wolfe being dead, and Gen. Monckton wounded, the command devolved upon Townshend, but Montcalm was unable to turn the incident to account, and, while attempting to rally a body of fugitive Canadians, near St. John's Gate, was mortally wounded. De Ramsay, who commanded the French garrison, asked his advice about defending the city, replied, "To your keeping I commend the honor of France. As for me, I must pass the night with God, and prepare myself for death." He died on the following day, and was buried within the precints of Ursuline Convent. His skull was dug up, a few years since, and placed in a glass case, and can now be seen by applying to the Chaplain of the convent. The remains of Wolfe were conveyed to England, and he was buried in a vault in the parish church of Greenwich. De Ramsay held out till the 17th of September, and then the French forces were surrendered.

In 1775 a small American force, under Gen. Montgomery attempted to capture Quebec, but failed, with the loss of 700 men, and their commander. The building in which he died is on St.

Louis street, just above the St. Louis Hotel, on the opposite side. He was buried in Quebec, but, in 1818 the State of New York caused his remains to be removed to New York and placed beneath the monument, erected by the United States, in front of St. Paul's church, on Broadway.

Montcalm's Headquarters—1759.

Quebec stands on the promontory known as Cape Diamond, and the most elevated point, the citadel, is 345 feet above the river. The old town was, until recently, surrounded by a wall, two and three-fourths miles in circuit, mounted with cannon, and having five gates. Since the withdrawal of the English troops they have been taken down, thus removing one of the peculiar features that gave Quebec so much interest. The Plains of Abraham, west of the city, the French Cathedral, the Seminary Chapel, where there are some old, and rare paintings, Durham Terrace, and Grand Battery, are objects of interest to the stranger. Other places of historic interest will be pointed out on inquiry at the Hotel. Opposite the St. Louis Hotel is located the building which was occupied by Montcalm as his headquarters during the siege of Quebec. There is only one first-class hotel in Quebec, and that is the St. Louis House, kept by Willis Russell,

FALLS OF MONTMORENCI.

where good accommodations can be had. It is in the immediate vicinity of all objects of interest.

FALLS OF MONTMORENCY.

The Falls of Montmorency are eight miles east of Quebec. The drive through St. Roch and Beauport to the falls is pleasant and interesting. The Calashes, with tourists going to the falls, the excellent road, the dwellings of the French working people, which make almost a continuous village, and the peculiar customs of the people invest the drive with more than ordinary interest. The little church, at Beauport, passed on the way, will attract the attention of the tourist. Similar ones will be noticed in the French settlements, in various places in Canada. Montmorency River is not large, and flows over a rocky bottom, and falls nearly into the St. Lawrence below. The water makes an almost perpendicular descent 240 feet, and although the volume of water is small, this is one of the most beautiful cataracts in the country. The view from the staircase, at the head of the fall, and, also, from the bed of the river below, is very fine. The best idea of its hight is had from below. The tourist will also notice Quebec from this point, which makes a beautiful appearance.

Church at Beauport.

DOWN THE ST. LAWRENCE.

Murray Bay, 95; River du Loup, 115; Tadousac, 140; Ha! Ha! Bay, 200 miles.

Falls of Montmorency.

THE St. Lawrence in front of Quebec presents an animated appearance. The European steamships, river steamers, ships from almost every port in the world, lumber rafts, the fleet ferry boats and the small sailing crafts make an interesting picture of busy life. Point Levi opposite Quebec, with its fortifications, the Isle of Orleans to the eastward, and Cape Ann on the north shore beyond the Falls of Montmorency, make a landscape that is unequaled. Having looked upon this, and seen the many objects of interest around Quebec the tourist will find his trip well rounded off by going down the St. Lawrence and up the famous Saguenay. The steamers sail at 7 o'clock, a. m., Tuesdays, Wednesdays, Thursdays and Fridays, on the arrival of the steamer from Montreal. Soon after leaving Quebec a good view of the Falls of Montmorency is had on the left.

THE ISLE OF ORLEANS.

Five miles below Quebec is the Isle of Orleans, discovered in 1535 by Jacques Cartier on his first voyage up the St. Lawrence, who named it Isle of Bacchus, on account of the great number of wild grape vines that he found upon the Island. It was subsequently named Isle of Orleans in honor of the Royal Family of France. It is 21 miles long and five broad. The Island is divided into small farms, narrow and long, extending from the shore to the center. The steamer passes the Island on the south side, following the regular ship channel. Below the Island, the river widens to twelve miles, and several small islands come in view, while Cape Tourment rises to the hight of 1800 feet.

GROSSE ISLE.

A few miles below the Isle of Orleans, and forty miles below Quebec, is Grosse Isle. This is quarantine grounds for the port of Quebec. More than twenty thousand emigrants have been buried here. On the south shore is St. Thomas. If the weather is favorable the steamer takes the north shore after passing the Isle of Orleans.

CRANE AND GOOSE ISLANDS.

Crane and Goose Islands are connected by a low marsh meadow. The islands were named from the fact that myriads of geese, ducks and teal inhabit them in the summer months. The river is here thirteen miles wide and is full of shoals. The channel is quite narrow and this is known to navigators as "The Traverse." The tide runs here at the rate of eight miles an hour.

North and easterly of Crane and Goose Islands are Race, Mill, Canoe, and Onion Islands, in the order named. Easterly and further north is Seal Island.

COUDRES ISLAND.

The steamer, if the weather is fine, usually keeps along the north shore, as the banks are more rugged and presents more picturesque beauty. If a fog prevails, it takes the regular ship channel on the south side. Coudres Island, which is the next to be passed, and close to the north shore, is the largest island in the St. Lawrence between the Isle of Orleans and the River Saguenay. It has indications of once having been joined to the main land and it is supposed to have slid off from it during some volcanic disturbance. The mountains on the north are quite prominent. Easterly of Coudres Island is Mt. Eboulemens, 2547 feet high. Coudres Island is owned by the priests of Lavel Seminary at Quebec. Passing Goose Cape the steamer enters Mal Bay.

MURRAY BAY.

After passing along Mal Bay, the steamer makes its first landing at Murray Bay. Here is a long and substantial wharf, built by the English government. This is quite a resort in summer for the wealthy people of Quebec and Montreal, and the many pe-

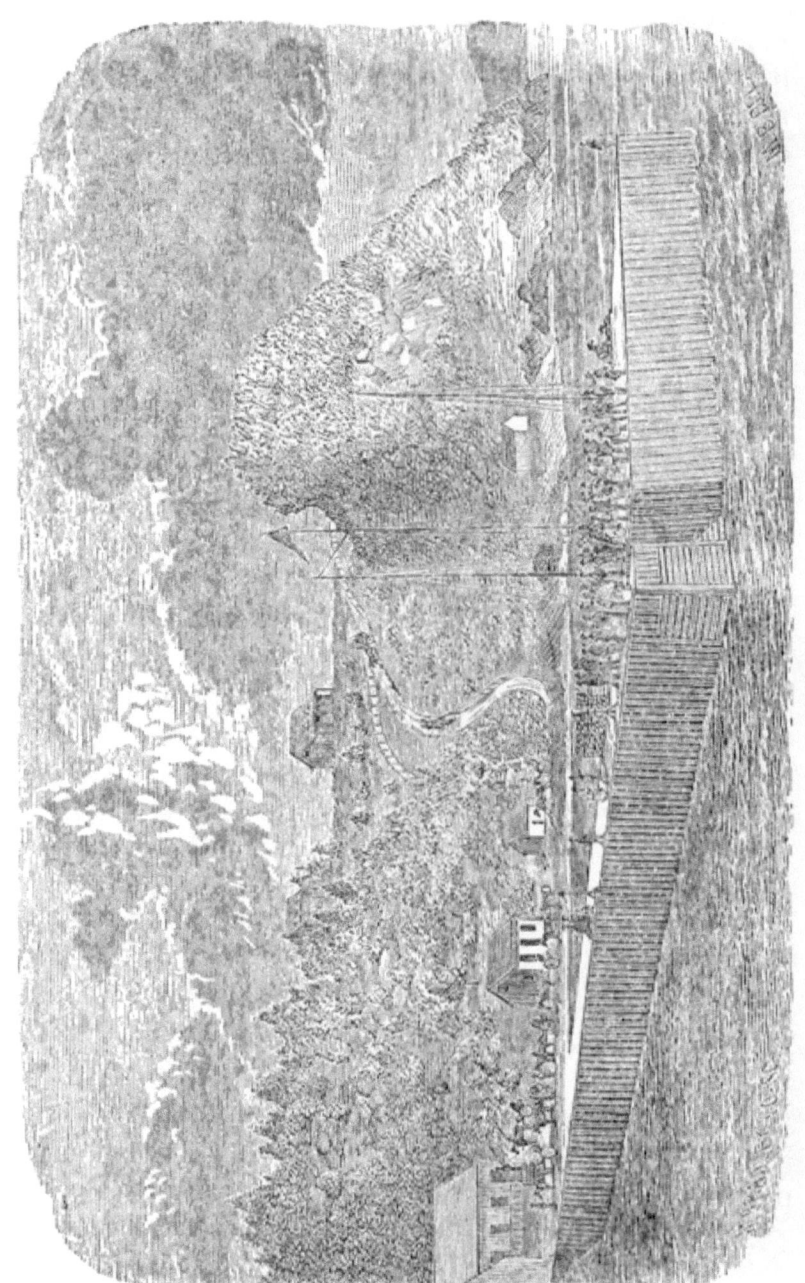

MURRAY BAY.

culiar vehicles that come down to the river present a novel appearance. The small village is about a mile from the river. Gen. Murray, one of the active commanders in the English army under Gen. Wolfe, during the siege of Quebec, came here with his Scotch Highland regiment, after the surrender of that city and settled. The soldiers finally married into the French families residing in this vicinity, and what is remarkable the Scotch element, in

THE CANADIAN CALASH.

course of time, has been completely obliterated, except in the mere names of their descendants. The tenacious Scotch Presbyterian has become a French Roman Catholic, losing not only his religion but his mother tongue. At the present time there will be found numerous families of McLeans, McDonalds and other well known Scotch names, who speak French and do not know a word of English. Another such a remarkable change of language and religion by intermarriage is not found on this Continent.

After leaving Murray Bay, the steamer takes a more southerly course, heading diagonally across the river for River du Loup. The small villages of Ouell, St. Anne, and Kamouraska have been noticed on the south shore, but the principal objects of interest are The Pilgrims, five rocky islands, which rise high above the water and present a novel appearance. A lighthouse, 180 feet high, has been established on Long Pilgrim.

THE PILGRIMS.

To the left and east of The Pilgrims is Hare Island. Near and just south of the easterly part of the Island is a small island with a lighthouse, which is known as the Brandy Pots. Here smugglers used to secrete their contraband liquors.

RIVER DU LOUP.

To the right and near at hand is River du Loup, the terminus of the River du Loup division of the Grand Trunk Railway, extending from Point Levi, opposite Quebec, and running parallel with the river, a mile or two to the south. Here is another long and substantial wharf, built by the English government. This is the landing for Cacona, the Newport of Canada. It is about four miles east of River du Loup and can be seen from the steamer. The wealthy people of Montreal and Quebec, come here to spend the summer and enjoy sea bathing.

On leaving River du Loup, the steamer heads northward for the mouth of River Saguenay. The

RIVER DU LOUP.

St. Lawrence here is twenty miles wide, and the north shore is only dimly seen. Green Island and its lighthouse will be seen to the eastward. North and in front of the mouth of the Saguenay is Red Island Light, 75 feet high. Passing this the entrance to the Saguenay comes in full view and in a short time the steamer is entering it. Tadousac will have been noticed upon the right bank overlooking the harbor and the St. Lawrence.

ENTRANCE TO THE SAGUENAY.

THE RIVER SAGUENAY.

Quebec, 140; Montreal, 320; Ha! Ha! Bay, 60; Cape Trinity, 30; Chicoutimi, 72 miles.

The Church at Tadousac.

THE entrance to the Saguenay presents a grand and beautiful appearance. The river is nearly a mile wide, and the mountains on either side are from six hundred to eleven hundred feet high. La Boule, a high rounded point upon the east side, but seemingly in the center of the river, adds beauty to the scene. The steamer sails up the river and makes a landing behind a high point just north of Tadousac. The boats reach this place just before sunset, and nothing can be more beautiful. The sides of the high cliffs are dark and somber, while the golden rays of the setting sun fall upon the water, and increase the beauty of this grand picture. The point opposite the landing is 1,100 feet high, while the lowest is not less than 700 feet. The steamer will remain here till 11 o'clock, and then proceed up the river at night, arriving at Ha! Ha! Bay about 6 o'clock the next morning.

Tadousac is an old trading post of the Hudson Bay Company, and their buildings are still standing. The Hotel near them is frequented by parties who come here to fish for salmon and enjoy the invigorating air. Here was held the first religious services by white men on this Continent; and the little Catholic church dates further back than any other in this country. Jacques Cartier entered this harbor Sept. 1, 1535, on his voyage up the St. Lawrence. He made a landing and held religious worship near where the church stands. There are some very fine paintings in the church, that are of great age, by artists long ago famous in the old world. Entrance can be obtained on inquiry at the Hotel. The stay here adds greatly to the trip up the Saguenay, as there is much here that is strange and interesting. Returning to the boat, after visiting the church, you retire for the night. About 11 o'clock the steamer resumes the trip up the river. The object of this is, to so divide the time as to approach the principal points of interest under the most favorable circumstances, and give a view of the entire route by daylight, either in going or returning.

The rivers flowing into the Saguenay are full of salmon, and gentlemen come here from great distances to enjoy the sport of taking them. The Saguenay is about a mile wide, and very deep, rarely less than 600 feet, and, in places, nearly one thousand.

About 6 o'clock, the next morning, the steamer approaches the landing at Ha! Ha! Bay. The sun has risen and casts its rays upon the water. To the left is Grand Bay and its little village. North is Ha! Ha! Bay and its little church, the principal object in every village in the French settlements. The settlers, who speak little but poor French, are crowding down to the wharf, anxious

ARRIVAL AT HA! HA! BAY.

to make a shilling, and, generally, they succeed in doing it. Late in the season, loads of blue berries, packed in peculiarly shaped wooden boxes, are brought down to the boat and shipped to Quebec and Montreal. The Calash drivers crowd around and solicit your patronage in broken English. As the steamer remains here till 10 o'clock, there is time for a ride to Grand Bay in the peculiar vehicle of this region, which is so antique and novel that you are induced to accept the offer, and nowhere can one get more sport for his money.

Ha! Ha! Bay is nearly at the head of steam navigation. The river comes into the bay at Cape East. Several miles above is Chicoutimi, a trading post of the Hudson Bay Company. Just above this point are the rapids, where the tides end. The spring tide at Ha! Ha! Bay rises to the hight of eighteen feet, sixty miles from the St. Lawrence.

GOING TO MARKET.

The Canadian French people are social in their habits and unlike the rural Yankee settle as near each other as possible. Their houses are in close proximity, while their farms extend backward from the street. This gives the French settlements the appearance of a continuous village. The dwellings are as near alike as two peas. Comfort and architectural beauty seems never to have been regarded in their construction. The necessities and not the luxuries of life are the only objects to be regarded. Much of the cooking and general work of the family are done out of doors. In every yard will be found the same looking oven and the same kettle suspended from a pole and in which boiling and cooking are done. Such simplicity is not found elsewhere.

The Canadian Oven.

The steamer commences the return trip at ten o'clock, and all the way down the river to Tadousac are points of great interest. The rocky Cliffs come down to the water and in places over-hang it. The rocks, mostly granite, are bare and resemble those in the White Mountain region. Here and there a cascade comes down the sides of the steep rocks and falls into the river. About an hour after leaving Ha! Ha! Bay, you come to the Tableaus, a perpendicular rock on the west side of the river. The steamer keeps close to the western shore and shortly afterward commences to round the point which brings in view

CAPES TRINITY AND ETERNITY.

These are the great objects of interest on the Saguenay. They present a perpendicular front of nearly 1800 feet. The steamer passes close in shore under cape Trinity and then the whistle is sounded.

CAPE TRINITY.

An echo comes back clear and distinct. The steamer remains here a short time and then slowly turns into the river and proceeds toward the St. Lawrence. There is nothing more grand on the Continent, and it is so unexpected, that the tourist is delighted and astonished. Trinity is named from the three well defined steps or notches in its northern side, first seen coming down the Saguenay. As the steamer passes out of Trinity Bay the Captain

ST. LOUIS ISLAND.

will point out the profile, on Cape Trinity. The water, at this point, is nearly 1,000 feet deep.

Keeping on down the river, River St. Jean and Little Saguenay are passed on the west side. Below them is St. Louis Island, directly in the center of the river and seemingly cutting off farther progress. Its well rounded and rocky sides make a beautiful appearance. Passing it, the onward course is pursued and late in the afternoon the St.

Lawrence is reached and as the view of the Saguenay recedes, you watch it with great interest, conscious of having looked upon the grandest water and mountain scenery in America.

The steamer touches at River du Loup and Murray Bay on the return trip and the next morning finds you at Quebec, fully satisfied with the tour.

www.ingramcontent.com/pod-product-compliance
Lightning Source LLC
Chambersburg PA
CBHW022057230426
43672CB00008B/1205